D1238393

Consecrated Venom

Caryl Johnston was born in 1947 in Birmingham, Alabama. She is the author of *Instead of Eyes* (1979), poems on Biblical themes, and *The Thoroughbred Colt: Identity and Moral Will in a Southern Family* (1999), a study of the impact of slavery, civil rights, and religion on one Southern family over five generations.

Caryl Johnston works as an editorial assistant at the University of Alabama.

Caryl Johnston

Consecrated Venom

The Serpent and the Tree of Knowledge

Floris Books

First published in 2000 by Floris Books

British Library CIP Data available

ISBN 0-86315-309-7

Printed in Great Britain
by Biddles Ltd, Guildford

Contents

Dedication and Acknowledgements

This book has been through many transformations since it began. I would like to thank my husband, Robert S. Horner, for his interest and unfailing sense of how it might be better. I dedicate this work to him and to our sons, Paul and Julian Horner.

Clifford Monks, Joseph F. Johnston, Jr., and Timothy Luke Johnson read earlier versions, and offered encouragement and suggestions for improvement. Frank Thielman read part of this manuscript and I appreciate his responses and scholarly annotations.

Sophronia Camp and Thomas Wilcox taught me an essential lesson about the 'ransoming process.' I wish to express my thanks to both of them.

I wish to thank Christopher J. Moore of Floris Books for his high standards, support, and encouragement. Without his inspired editorial supervision this book never would have happened.

Caryl Johnston
Birmingham, Alabama
December 6, 1999

Moses lifted up the serpent in the wilderness ...
John 3:14

Introduction

Biblical Religion or Biblical Epistemology?

The Bible is the main source of the religious tradition in the West. This Judeo-Christian tradition resolves into the two religions, Judaism and Christianity, with their innumerable tributaries: churches, synagogues, denominations, sects, movements, branches, and offshoots.

When we examine the word, *religion,* we make an interesting discovery. Most commonly, we are apt to hear that the word, *religion,* derives from the Latin, *religare,* to bind or to link, hence meaning the bond between man and God. This meaning is given in the *Oxford Dictionary of English Etymology,* which can certainly be considered a reliable authority. This is the meaning which is most often cited when defining the term, *religion.*

However, let us keep digging. There was another etymological dictionary published in Oxford, the *Etymological Dictionary of the English Language,* compiled by the Rev Walter Skeat. This work gives a more comprehensive view of our word, and indeed it contradicts the previous etymology. The definition reads as follows:

RELIGION, piety, the performance of duties to God and man ... Allied to *religens,* fearing the gods, pious. [And therefore not derived from religare, to bind.] The opposite of *negligens,* negligent; see *Neglect.* Allied also to *diligens,* diligent ... Thus *religion* and *neglect* are from the same root *leg–* which also appears in Gk. *alegein,* to have a care for, to heed ... etc.

Thus we have two etymological meanings of *religion:*
(1) that which binds or links man to the divine world;
(2) care and attention to the relationship with God.

In the first meaning, we may assume that what binds or links us to the divine world is religious ritual. Religious ritual returns us to the origins — of the world and mankind — and through ritual we commemorate this origin, the beginning of things.

Usually, discussions of religious ritual then go on to say how the story of the world's origins is recapitulated in the ritual. The sources of the ritual are discussed; its links to mythology are brought out; its sociological, economic, or historical function is illuminated. These scholarly contributions are important and fruitful, but basically, such discussions leave one with the impression that ritual is but one more phenomenon in the world which it is possible to write books about, keep a safe distance from, understand at light years away from one's own moral development.

In this book it is the second meaning of the word, religion, that I wish to explore. I intend to argue that religious ritual, or revelation, has to do with the act of thinking — and that this thinking is inescapably involved with our moral development — with who, and what, we are. In this essay I argue that religious ritual commemorates the act of thinking, which in its most fundamental mode is paying attention.

Religious revelation, which is the source of religious ritual, has to do with *the act of paying attention to what thinking is.*

But this *act of paying attention to thinking* which is the substance of revelation and which is commemorated in religious ritual is not the 'paying attention' that the anthropologist tells us about. The anthropologist speaks of early man and says that he paid attention when he saw the leaves moving nearby, thus inferring that a tiger was lurking under the bush about ready to spring at him. The anthropologist says that man pays attention in order to survive.

The issue here is not prehistorical tigers or modern traffic signals. Obviously, we pay attention in order to survive. It's a commonsense proposition: survival skills are necessary if we are to survive.

The anthropologist cannot explain why human beings would

pay attention for the sake of paying attention, why a human being would enter a state of attentive thinking (thinking for its own sake; contemplation) when there is no tiger in the immediate vicinity. Or maybe, even if there is.

Furthermore, I argue that this paying-attention-to-what-thinking-is embodies an impulse or spur to action — and perhaps to a much greater extent than just paying attention in order to survive. People who pay attention to survive, usually survive. People who pay attention to thinking do more than survive. They make history possible. That is, they take survival to another level. They raise it into a mode of being which, as far as we know, may be unique in the universe: a mode which embraces the universal and the particular by means of action, consequence, development, transformation, change, metamorphosis, tradition, continuity, and innovation.

This book is about paying attention to the act of thinking with respect to the Bible, especially the Creation story in Genesis.

I think that Genesis contains an unusually rich model or example of thinking-about-thinking.

Once I realized that there was a new way to understand the Creation story, once I saw that it was possible to have a vital relation to this document by pondering what happens when we think, I discovered that this idea — the connection between Genesis and thinking — was absolutely novel, if not foreign, to our culture. Popular presentations of Biblical ideas, not to mention the presentation of these ideas in the churches, so often seemed to me to lack this dimension of vital knowing. The Bible, in the churches or in books or on television, was most often presented without any cognitive or epistemological focus at all. Is it any wonder that so many people should find the Bible incoherent, mythological, irrelevant to modern concerns, a power or patriarchal narrative?

For example, in Karen Armstrong's 'new interpretation of Genesis,' *(In the Beginning)* there is little of what could be called the cognitive dimension. It is a moral and psychological reading of the Creation text. Armstrong recognizes the complexity of the biblical story and makes a plug for imaginative effort in understanding it. But after this warning, blandness and superficiality take over. 'People,' she says, 'originally turned to religion because they wanted to live as intensely and efficaciously as possible.'

Even so, the people in Genesis did not live 'intensely and efficaciously' according to Armstrong. Noah just wanted to save his own skin from the Flood, and Isaac 'is yet another of the survivors of Genesis who found it impossible to integrate past trauma.' Here is a Genesis dressed up in the robes of victimhood and survivorship — Genesis as False Memory Syndrome. Unfortunately for God and biblical characters, there is no court of law to which they may resort to clear their names from this poisonous atmosphere of false accusations. There could be no reading of Genesis more opposed to its spirit than this.

Better, though not by much, were discussions on Bill Moyers' television program on the Abraham-Isaac story in Genesis. For the scholars gathered on that program, the Bible, where it was not a text preaching social justice, remained at a safe distance from the teachers and professors presumably hired to teach it. Not a single Western scholar, Jewish or Christian, dealt with the Bible's implications for *thinking*. There was hardly a hint that the Bible might be a text that demanded something from us — some effort, some moral demand. The one exception to the panel was a Muslim, who spoke out of an intelligent and passionate conviction about the moral demands of monotheism. His honesty was refreshing in contrast to the predictable intellectualisms of the comfortable and the jaded.

Of much more intellectual substance is Andrew Delbanco's book, *The Death of Satan: How Americans Have Lost the Sense of Evil.* Although this book is not directly concerned with biblical matters, it deals with spheres of belief that derive from the biblical heritage. Delbanco's concern is the absence of religious or metaphysical belief in general — the void of moral knowledge in the modern world. He says: 'We have reached a point where it is not only specific objects of belief that have been discredited but the very capacity to believe ... In the past, when the old ways of seeing the world gave way, it was possible to discern at least the outlines of a new way that would take their place ... But the process we are living through is sufficiently different in degree that it has become different in kind ... It is divestiture without reinvestment.'

In Delbanco's view, the absence of religious or metaphysical convictions has created a situation of historical, or spiritual, stagnation. This is an important point, and one to which I will return in later chapters. But for now I want to observe that I think Delbanco does speak truly about the nature of belief. It is now no longer enough just to believe. By talking about the figure of Satan — real or mythological — Delbanco suggests that an 'epistemological hole' has appeared in the place that God once occupied. As Dostoevsky put it, 'If God is dead, everything is permitted.' If God is not real, evil is. 'Evil will have become an epistemological problem. This is the vanishing point to which we seem headed.'

Andrew Delbanco has taken this riddle of the Modern Age — the problem of evil — profoundly to heart. But he is a diagnostician, not a healer. Is there a way to get out of this impasse — the abyss brought on by 'God is dead'? Is there a way to cross over to the other side of the abyss?

This essay is an attempt to get to the other side: to wrest from the Bible and history a new understanding — a reinvestment.

* * * *

This thinking-about-thinking in the Bible I call 'biblical epistemology.' As I will argue, in biblical epistemology we have an impulse toward development and participation by human beings.

This development and participation by human beings is called, in the Old Testament, the Covenant.[1] In the New Testament, attention is given to the idea of the 'parabolic utterance' — the kind of receptive speaking and hearing it is necessary to possess in order to participate in the covenant.[2]

Classical philosophy, too, possesses the participatory element. It is called dialectic, the art of critical disputation or examination into the truth of an idea or opinion. As practised by Socrates and recorded by Plato, the dialectic had elements of conversation, verbal, logical and psychological analysis, news reportage, storytelling, and poetic composition.

The participation idea was important in the Middle Ages, most notably in the practice of the religious ritual of the Communion, but also with scholastic philosophy.[3] With the increasing secularization of society, however, participation became increasingly important as a political idea. It begins to emerge in ideas about democracy and human equality. Not only did modern political movements incorporate the utopian imagination in their visions of the future, but as was becoming increasingly evident, participation in the culture itself demanded the quality of imagination. One of the more striking developments in modernity is this polarizing of the idea of Imagination into 'left-wing' (utopian or political) and 'right-wing' (conservative or literary) branches.

Thus Russell Kirk, whose book *The Conservative Mind* revitalized the modern American conservative tradition, hearkened back to Edmund Burke, who coined the phrase 'moral imagination.' Burke was an author and political speaker who strongly condemned the French revolutionaries of his time for attempting to remould society along the lines of a rationalist utopia. Russell Kirk helped to carry on in literature what Edmund Burke began in political speculation. Writing about himself in his autobiographical book, *The Sword of Imagination,* Kirk remarked that: 'He meant to wake the moral imagination through the evocative power of humane letters.'[4]

Likewise Owen Barfield, an English solicitor — the friend of C.S. Lewis, J.R.R. Tolkien, Charles Williams — whose book, *Saving the Appearances* calls for the education of the imagination and intellect so that we moderns, in general so alienated from the grand mansions of Tradition, will be able to understand history anew as an evolution in consciousness. This renewed understanding Barfield calls 'final participation.'

And this book, *Saving the Appearances,* has had no more than a minute, even hidden, impact upon modern intellectual life. But where its message has been digested, that impact has been pure, powerful, and even life-changing. The historian John Lukacs once said that this book is among the most important to appear in our time. He cites Barfield in his own magisterial work, *Historical Consciousness.* In this work the 'evolution of consciousness' idea appears as 'the historical form of reconstruction ... [which] is one of the few things nowadays that can give people a particular mental connection with reality.'[5]

In this sketch of the participatory idea, we see how we have landed right back in our historical situation. John Lukacs boldly takes the idea of the developing, participating imagination back to epistemology when he says, in the 1985 edition of the work, that '... we must begin thinking, not about ideas, but about thinking itself.'

In my view, this development of the participation idea has come full circle. We are back to where we started: with the biblical Covenant.

Why the Bible — why the Covenant — rather than classical philosophy?

For there is another model about thinking: a thinking-about the world, the self, ethics, even about thinking itself. We are more familiar with this strand of thinking through the classical philosophical tradition that emerged from ancient Greece. We call this strand philosophy, and include by the term metaphysics, ethics, ontology, and epistemology. This strand of thinking is not at all times hostile to the concrete, relational, and participatory thrust of the first model of thinking. But it has tended to veer more into the direction of abstract universalism, and, as we all know, it has culminated with the Scientific Revolution and the highly technological world that we know today.

An excellent summation of this strand of thinking is the following:

> The grand narrative of modernity, evolving out of the scientific revolution of the sixteenth and seventeenth centuries, gradually entranced the Judeo-Christian West with the humanistic notion that the world is completely knowable through the application of human rationality and the scientific method and that material and moral progress would be the certain results of scientific rationalism. As the grand narrative unfolded in succeeding centuries, the importance of individualism and of free inquiry became attached to the modernist dogma.[6]

'The grand narrative of modernity' has emphasized the thinking-about-the world. The biblical narrative emphasizes the paying-attention-to-thinking, the thinking-about-thinking.

I have, of course, simplified. These two different kinds of thinking are not really so distinct, and in many cases they overlap, blend into each other, draw upon each other.

And yet, and yet ... with the biblical narrative we are already in a different world. It is a world in which thinking cannot be divorced from moral presence, urgency, consequence. It is the world of Temptation and Fall. It is the world of the Serpent.

For in the Bible there are actually two serpents. One of these serpents appears on the staff of Moses and seems to be connected with inspiration. The other serpent — the one we hear about — tempted Eve.[7]

The serpent of the Temptation represents the malignant intention to deceive. Misfortune, misapprehension, isolation, follow in the wake of this Serpent.

The serpent of inspiration leads to eloquence, community, dynamic historical development.

Can we find premonitory evidence of the two different kinds of thinking in the biblical picture of these two serpents?

This question will occupy our first chapter.

If you are interested in
other publications from
Floris Books, please
return this card with your
name and address.

I am interested in
following subjects:

- [ ] C Celtic
- [ ] R Religion
- [ ] S Science
- [ ] H Health & parenting
- [ ] J Children's books
- [ ] A Crafts & activities

PC-9804

Name _____
                              Surname

Address _____

_____

_____
                              Postcode

- [ ] Please send me your catalogue once
- [ ] Please send me your catalogue regularly

If you are in North America, our distributor, Anthroposophic
Press, will send their catalogue to you.

I found this card in: _____
                                    Book title

Postcard

Floris Books
15 Harrison Gardens
Edinburgh
EH11 1SH
Great Britain

Chapter One

The Serpent

*And the Lord God planted a garden eastward in Eden;
and there he put the man whom he had formed. And out
of the ground made the Lord God to grow every tree
that is pleasant to the sight, and good for food; the tree
of life also in the midst of the garden, and the tree of
knowledge of good and evil ...*

*And the Lord God commanded the man, saying, Of
every tree of the garden thou mayest freely eat; But of
the tree of knowledge of good and evil, thou shalt not
eat of it: for in the day that thou eatest thereof thou
shalt surely die.*   *Gen.2:8–9, 16–17*

*Now the serpent was more subtil than any beast of the
field which the Lord God had made. And he said unto
the woman, Yea, hath God said, Ye shall not eat of every
tree of the garden?*

*And the woman said unto the serpent, We may eat of
the fruit of the trees of the garden: But of the fruit of the
tree that is in the midst of the garden, God hath said, Ye
shall not eat of it, neither shall ye touch it, lest ye die.*

*And the serpent said unto the woman, Ye shall not
surely die. For God doth know that in the day that ye
eat thereof, then your eyes shall be opened, and ye shall
be as gods, knowing good and evil.*   *Gen.3:1–5*

*Of Man's first disobedience and the fruit
Of that forbidden tree whose mortal taste
Brought death into the world and all our woe ...*
                            Milton, Paradise Lost

The Serpent of Temptation

... One evening at the twilight
the serpent coiled himself upon the roots.
Rings of fire glittered round his navel,
from his eyes gleamed decay of light ...
                                        Four Rivers in Eden

The first cognitive act in the Bible is set in the frame of temptation and disobedience. Alternatively, an act of will involves a
cosmic moral transgression which leads to knowledge, enlighten-
ment, having one's 'eyes opened.'

Whether the Fall was an act of will or an act of thought: even
of this we cannot be too sure. Ambiguity meets us in the beginning, almost like a snake sliding along the ground, wrapping itself around the trunk of what we consider our inmost 'Selfhood,'
glaring at us in the sometimes harsh light of our own lives.

The serpent presses Eve with a remorseless logic. He contradicts God by saying that if she eats of the fruit of the tree of
knowledge, she will not die. Instead, if the humans eat of it, their
eyes will be opened, they will be as gods, they will know good
and evil.

This is a highly abstract discussion, a bringing of concepts to a
human being who cannot yet conceive, a human being who has
no experiential content for these abstractions. Contradiction,
death, opening of the eyes! What does it all mean? What is the
sense of the prohibition to Adam and Eve, how can they 'grasp
what death is, what good and evil are, living as [they] do in unbroken obedience to the Creator? Can all this mean anything to
[them] except empty words?'[1]

In contrast to the wisdom offered by the fruit from the tree of
knowledge, God's command not to eat of it may be interpreted as
an exaltation of experience for its own sake: not to subordinate
any experience for the sake of another — not even for wisdom —
not to shortchange our experience by calling it good or evil beforehand, before we have experienced it. God speaks for the

distinctiveness of each experience, of each creation, of each moment. Is it not true that the fruit from the tree of life is freely available? And that this fruit, being universal, would encompass all knowledge? That knowledge can be had by means of life, but not if it is grasped directly as knowledge? And why are Adam and Eve allowed to eat of the fruit of the tree of life, but not of the fruit of the tree of knowledge?

What is knowledge apart from life? Leo Strauss remarks that 'The Bible rejects the principle of autonomous knowledge and everything that goes along with it.'[2] Autonomous knowledge — this is knowledge apart from life, knowledge for the sake of consumption, for the sake of the self, knowledge removed from the context in which it is embedded, in which it has meaning ... knowledge for the sake of knowledge.

But even the phrase, 'autonomous knowledge,' possesses something of a contradiction, an ambiguity. Autonomy has been a central preoccupation of modernity and of modern philosophy. No doubt it has been carried to absurd lengths: the human being can remove himself only so far from family, tribe, religion, regional history and social identity before he hits quicksand and his flounderings begin to resemble ever more elaborate attempts to re-invent the wheel. What begins as freedom ends as a waste of time.

Still, this preoccupation with autonomy and autonomous knowledge is not, in my view, wholly unbiblical. I think the Bible warns us that 'autonomous knowledge' is dangerous — that we must tread with caution — and if our eyes are to be opened then we must realize that death is at our shoulder.

Strauss's formulation, then, is too summary. If the Bible rejected the principle of autonomous knowledge and everything that goes along with it as summarily as he suggests, there could be no story of development. This 'story of development' is called, in theological language, *redemption*. Strauss's formulation undercuts the Bible as the great document of developing human freedom.

And furthermore: Paradise is a more complicated place than it first appears. For after all, God has permitted evil to exist, and evil is walking around in the guise of an 'angel of light' — the

Tempter, the serpent. The story seems to be as much of a warning
as a relation or narrative of something that happened. The warning is that human beings are unprotected with respect to the act of
knowing, that the Paradise that seems to shelter them cannot shelter them. It is not only that knowledge is dangerous. Even Paradise is dangerous. It is a cosmos, not just a garden, and a cosmos
has all kinds of beings in it. Not all of them are friendly to
humankind. As the Tempter promises: '... ye shall be as gods!'
Indeed. Can humanity possibly 'be as gods' — that is, know in
advance what kind of world they will unleash through their acts
of knowing?

And what kind of knowledge is 'knowledge in advance'? There
is no such thing, there can be no such thing, where human historical reality is concerned. The Temptation story, planted in the
midst of the garden, 'eastward of Eden,' soon begins to grow, to
take on the dimensions of human history. For soon that unpre-
dictable world of history breaks in. It is the world of action and
consequence and experience. Everything up until this point is
prophetic warning.

What is it that the Tempter offers us, that God says we are better off to decline? Perhaps it is that attitude toward life-experience
that would refuse the gift of something being what it is. Something else, another gift, is wanted. And yet why, in creation, is another thing wanted?

> The full inconceivability of this act is expressed ... by the
> fact that it is not an evil force from somewhere or other
> that suddenly breaks forth into creation. No, this evil is
> completely hidden within the world of creation and occurs
> in the creation through man ... the unadorned biblical
> account says in fact that the Fall was prepared and took
> place in the midst of creation, and it is just by this means
> that its complete inexcusability is expressed in the plainest
> possible way.[3]

In the world of creation, man's relation to knowledge is the inexplicable, the inexcusable. And in the world that still is creation, but has become an historical world, this relation continues

to be inexplicable and inexcusable. 'Error is the price we pay for progress,' remarked Alfred North Whitehead. It is the recognition that the tree of knowledge remains outside of us eternally and simultaneously at the 'edge of history' and within the heart of man.

The Serpent of Inspiration

> *And Moses answered and said, But, behold, they will not believe me, nor hearken unto my voice: for they will say, The LORD hath not appeared unto thee.*
>
> *And the LORD said unto him, What is that in thine hand? And he said, A rod.*
>
> *And he said, Cast it on the ground. And he cast it on the ground, and it became a serpent; and Moses fled before it.*
>
> *And the LORD said unto Moses, Put forth thine hand, and take it by the tail.' And he put forth his hand, and caught it; and it became a rod in his hand.*
>
> *That they may believe that the Lord God of their fathers, the God of Abraham, the God of Isaac, the God of Jacob, hath appeared unto thee.*   *Exod.4:1–5*

In the Gospel of John, in the New Testament, there is an interesting conversation between Jesus and Nicodemus. Nicodemus was an important figure of his time, a member of the Jewish Sanhedrin. Evidently he had been curious about the teachings of this young rabbi, Jesus, and he had come to see him and question him. This particular conversation between Jesus and Nicodemus became important in Christian history, for during the course of it, Jesus, in response to a question by Nicodemus, replied that to enter the kingdom of the Spirit you had to be 'born again.'

But it is not this passage that attracted my attention, but rather another phrase that Jesus utters a few moments later in the course of trying to explain to Nicodemus what he means by the phrase, 'born again.' Nicodemus had taken Jesus' words literally, and had asked whether to be 'born again' meant that a man had literally to re-enter his mother's womb a second time. Jesus tells him, no, it's

not like that; the things of the mind and spirit are not like the
things of the flesh. All of a sudden Jesus mentions the mysterious
phrase, the 'Son of Man.' He says that no one can ascend to the
heavenly realm except he who came down from heaven, 'even as
the Son of Man which is in heaven.'

It is possible to feel sympathy for Nicodemus' bewilderment.
But then comes the kicker. Jesus says: 'And as Moses lifted up the
serpent in the wilderness, even so must the Son of Man be lifted
up.' (John 3:14)

What is going on here? Aside from the oft-debated question of
the meaning of the term, 'Son of Man,' why does Jesus refer to
Moses and the serpent? The question intrigued me. I own a
Scofield Reference Bible, which gives cross-references to important passages in the Bible. According to a note in this edition, I
was referred to a passage in the Old Testament, Exodus 4:15. In
this chapter, God is telling Moses about his mission and trying to
persuade him to accept it. God performs signs to convince Moses
to accept his task and lead the children of Israel out of Egypt.

In one of these signs, God changes the staff of Moses into a serpent, and then back again into a staff. Yet Moses still complains
to God about his lack of eloquence, and God says to him: 'I will
be with thy mouth, and will teach you what ye shall do.'

This vivid, concentrated picture of the serpent held up in the
wilderness — the rod changed into the serpent and changed back
again to a rod — struck me as a good emblem for this book. The
serpent power is connected with the idea of inspiration and eloquence in speaking. God gives to Moses the power to transform
the serpent, and this is the power that gives Moses the certainty
and confidence to accept his mission.

There is a curious aspect to this conjunction of the serpent-
power with the act of speech. Most people who are familiar with
Eastern spiritual practice have heard of the *kundalini,* the power-
force that originates in the base of the spine and travels up the
spine, like lightning, when released in meditation.

The picture in Exodus is a very different kind of kundalini. The
kundalini of Moses — to put it that way — works not from the
bottom up, but from the top down. It is connected with the brain,
with speaking, with eloquence, with the power to inspire and to

lead. It becomes an instrument of transformation and dynamic change. It works from the top down — from the mind to the body of mankind in history.

I believe this change of direction is an important clue to Western spirituality. Spirituality in the West begins with intelligence. Spiritual activity begins with thinking activity. Thus the serpent has pointed us to thinking and cognition. What is it about the serpent that it should lead us in this direction?

Knowing the Serpent

Why does God use the serpent to empower Moses in the Book of Exodus, when in the Book of Genesis it is the serpently creature who beguiles and deceives Eve? Does the creature possess magic powers of its own, or are its powers evoked according to who uses them and for what purpose? How can a Being who in Genesis 3 evidently possesses a will of its own (and a malignant will at that) become a symbol of power in Exodus? Is the snake a power or the symbol of the misuse of power?

Serpent or snake symbolism is fundamental in myth and history. Brewer's Dictionary of Phrase and Fable mentions six different symbolisms of the serpent, as follows:

1. Symbol of deity or God: because '... it feeds upon its own body; even so, all things spring from God and will be resolved into deity again ...' (Plutarch)
2. Eternity, corollary to deity: because the serpent is often represented as forming a circle, holding its tail in its mouth.
3. Renovation, healing and medical practice: Thus Brewer's: 'It is said that when old it has the power of growing young again "like the eagle," by casting its slough, which is done by squeezing itself between two rocks.' The caduceus, symbol of healing, was a white wand around which two serpents were depicted. The serpent was sacred to Aesculapius, Greek god of medicine —

though most often the cock was sacrificed to this god, as
one may recall through the last poignant words of
Socrates: 'I owe a cock to Aesculapius.'
4. Guardian spirit: The figure of a serpent was often depicted on Greek and Roman altars.
5. Wisdom: 'Be ye therefore wise as serpents, and harmless
as doves.' Matt.10:16
6. Subtlety: 'Now the serpent was more subtle than any
beast ...' etc. Gen.3:1

The connection between the serpent and the eagle is not farfetched morphologically. Hermann Poppelbaum writes that zool-
ogists find a connection between birds and reptiles and stresses
that 'the way towards the snake form must be viewed as the coun-
termove to the contrasting ascent of the other reptile families and
genera toward the realm of the birds.'[4] Poppelbaum's descriptions
of the snake are worth quoting at length:

... The *true Snakes* are anatomically characterized by their
lidless eyes and by the single band-like row of scales along
their undersides ...
    The trunk principle has become supreme. The weird
dissolution of the skeleton into a loose chain ... engulfs
even the skull ... The jaw elements can move against each
other like the levers and shafts of a machine ... Since both
halves of the jaws can move independently, the snake, in
the act of swallowing, can press the fangs of one side into
its victim while the other side loosens its grip and moves
forward. The chewing is here a kind of walking ...
    The absence of the middle ear and drum means that the
whole body transmits sound ...
    Something extraordinary must be said about the *eyes* of
the snakes. The lids are closed and grown together, but
they have become as transparent as glass. Behind them a
space has arisen that is filled with tears, thus formed a
secondary lens in front of the true eye. *Thus the snake is
able to see through its closed lids* (Italics his).
    ... Whatever region they inhabit, the snakes use the same

winding form of locomotion. Creeping on the ground, swimming in the water, climbing in trees, even jumping through the air, is the same gesture for them. They treat all elements as if they were not yet divided. They behave as if the structure of nature's kingdoms still lingered on in an ancient chaotic phase. Indeed, the snakes have never actually set foot on the earth.[5]

Serpentine Duplicity and Moral Imagination

Even to read the scientific description of the serpent is to succumb to fascination. Something about the snakes reminds us of human intuitive or imaginative capacity, such as their winding gesture which treats 'all elements as if they were not yet divided,' their seeing through (tearful!) lidded eyes, even their transmission of sound through their whole body. Everything seems oriented towards hearing and swallowing. The snakes seem to be an odd combination of high-strung, shrinking sensitivity and angry, aggressive striking. We flee from them; they flee from us. Yet the encounters between human and snake have an element of the archetypal, the epic — and, in the case of poisonous varieties — the potentially fatal.

Even today, when *participation mystique* has virtually been eradicated in the human being's relation to nature, the snake evokes a fundamental chord, a sounding-together of the natural and the moral. There is something morally repellent in the snake, at least for most people. This feeling may not apply to the friendly blacksnake who helps keep down the rat population. But for poisonous snakes whose whip-lashing tongue may eject venomous substance into our blood: here is something we can't quite get over. The venomous snake forces us to pack up and vacate our house of moral neutrality. The venom of the snake forces us out of the lukewarm, the complacent, the comfortable. In this sense the snake is an apocalyptic creature, in his stubborn and even perverse way a partner with the God who in Revelation condemns the Laodicean humanity: '... because thou art lukewarm, and neither cold nor hot, I will spew thee out of my mouth' (Rev.3:16).

This 'doubleness' or 'diabolism' in the snake even appears in what, in man, is the organ of speaking: the tongue. The famous 'forked tongue' of serpentine duplicity is a counter-image to the Pentecostal 'speaking in tongues' which was the inspirational founding of the early Christian church (Acts 2:3).

The serpent of religion, science, history, and myth provides much provision to our armoury of imagination. But as Owen Barfield reminds us, 'imagination and goodness are *not* synonymous.'[6]

Indeed, the promise of the Tempter — that by eating of the forbidden fruit humankind would be 'as gods,' knowing good and evil — seems to be true of the serpent itself. The theme of doubleness plays in endless variations. This 'doubleness' even applies to the *name,* or rather, *names,* of the Tempter. As Andrew Delbanco remarks in *The Death of Satan,* '... there was no sacred text in the Judeo-Christian tradition that exhibited him [i.e. Satan] with entire clarity.' He is called, variously, Lucifer, Beelzebub, Belial, Mammon. And doubtless there are other names. Among modern spiritual researchers, Rudolf Steiner (1861–1925) clarified the 'doubleness' of this Tempter by formulating the two names — Lucifer and 'Ahriman'— the Persian name for Satan. We will have occasion later in this book to make concrete use of Steiner's clarification. In the story of the *Akedah,* or 'Binding' of Isaac, Steiner's insight into the nature of *diaballein* — the Devil — becomes remarkably fruitful.

F. Scott Fitzgerald once remarked that, 'the test of a first-rate intelligence is the ability to hold two opposed ideas in the mind at the same time, and still retain the ability to function.' The poet John Keats also said something similar in his characterization of the 'negative capability' of the poetic sensibility. It subsists with sureness and unsureness, of not always having to be irritably reaching out after fact and truth.

Notice that both of these statements bring us into a realm of doubleness, of something that could, in other circumstances, be close to 'serpentine duplicity.'

Yet both have to do with mind and character, and both seem to involve a kind of 'two-step' or double movement.[7] The weak person, or really any one of us in moments of weakness, has a vivid internal drama going on. Duplicity is a kind of gravitational unsoundness. Weakness attaches itself to the eccentric element in imagination, to this propensity to treat all elements 'as if they lingered on in an ancient chaotic phase.' A more solidified mental life, on the other hand, undergirds the moral imagination. Persons able to tolerate paradox have harnessed themselves to the forces of gravity in this sense. This gravity, despite its connotations with weight and heaviness, keeps things aloft and on course. Those who are open to the unceasing tug-of-war between certainty and doubt can hear this music of the spheres.

Thinking About Participation

These metaphors from astronomy are appropriate to begin a discussion of participation. For thousands of years, people observed the movements of the heavenly bodies. The observed regularity in these movements led to the development of mathematical thinking and science. The harmonies of celestial movements became those 'appearances' which referred back to the *phainomena* of the sixth century Simplicius.[8]

Yet in translating the steps of the celestial dance into mathematics, science was almost too successful. In the early modern period — from about the 1600s on — the actual steps of the process, a kind of dance involving the observation of natural regularities and human cognition, became 'swallowed up' in a mathematized and mechanized view of nature. The human participation was discounted, as if to suggest that human beings, having performed the cognitive work creditably, could go sit in the sidelines and merely watch the spectacle.

It is not that modern persons do not 'participate' in nature or even in the scientific view of nature. But the links between this participation and vital cultural expressions grow ever more impoverished. Modern culture has an increasingly 'synthetic' and artificial character. 'Virtual reality' is only the latest expression of this development, a truly ripe fruit of the unreal.

Much is at stake here, and not only 'participation' in a merely
political or social sense. In the long run, Barfield warns: '... we
shall not be able to save souls without saving the appearances,
and it is an error fraught with the most terrible consequences to
imagine that we shall.'[9] In a cosmos in which human being do not
appear to participate, it is no great leap to say it is a cosmos in
which human beings merely *appear by chance.* Somehow, there
is a disproportion between the argument that we all arrived here
by accident and the spectacle of scientists writing great tomes to
prove it. In the late twentieth century, often even serious intellectual life has this quality of giddiness — of the 'unbearable light-
ness of being' (Kundera).

In summarizing his argument, Barfield shows how the development of objective science accompanies the growth of a 'spec-
tator' or non-participating consciousness. But the step from an
evolution of consciousness to *historical* consciousness — which
is not the 'history of consciousness' as such as it is the realization
of our historical condition and the implications of this realization
for our thinking — this is the step for biblical epistemology to
take.

This 'historical consciousness' is summed up by John Lukacs
when he says that *'history, for us, has become a form of thought'*[10]
(Italics his). For to be sure, empirical reasoning and objective
science are also 'forms of thought.' Both historical consciousness
and objective science are forms of thought that are 'dictated by
the way things are' (Polkinghorne). But the personal and partici-
pant character of historical knowledge means that history cannot
be a 'science' in the sense in which that word is ordinarily used.
John Lukacs adds a new dimension to the concept of 'modernity'
when he sums up his project in the following terms:

> ... I believe that the most important developments in our
> civilization during the last three or four centuries include
> not only the applications of scientific method but also the
> growth of historical consciousness; and that while we may
> have exaggerated the importance of the former we have
> not yet understood sufficiently the implications of the
> latter.[11]

Genuine modernity is no longer science. Genuine modernity is historical consciousness.

* * * *

What does all of this have to do with the serpent?

Taking the serpent as a powerful and compressed symbol of human imaginative and cognitive capacity, we see at once our great opportunity and our great danger. In recapitulating the cognitive steps, in learning about science once again through history, we expose ourselves to a new dimension of risk-taking and responsibility. The old world picture, which we viewed from the sidelines, seems distant, half-baked, and dull. We have been restored to the centre where drama and action take place. After all, it is our world, the world in which human beings have come to exist. This is a world no longer casual and accidental. Our eyes have been opened indeed. Whether we become entranced by the Serpent who freezes us or activated by the Serpent who inspires us is our decision.

These thoughts will accompany us as we plunge ahead into the mysteries of biblical epistemology, which more than any other epistemology, takes account of time and the earth — the coming into incarnation of the human intelligence.

Chapter Two

It Is That It Is

Thought and Personal Being

In the beginning God created heaven and earth.
Gen.1:1.

'The Bible begins in a place where our thinking is at its most passionate.' This statement by Dietrich Bonhoeffer is a good place from which to approach the first line of the Creation story. If we allow the Creation story to work on us, if we put away our preconceptions about it, our secular-culture-derived bias against it (as also our fundamentalist-culture-derived bias in favour of it) we perceive that we are brought forward, or immersed, in a world situation empty of almost everything except personal being. In this way the statement, so concise as to resemble an equation, and which mentions a number of things (four or five), puts us into an immediate, urgent and passionate relation with a personal being.

This personal being is unknown, except as the author of Genesis gives it the name, 'God.' Thus indirectly we know that man is present, because God is named, and yet the narrative proceeds to tell us how God creates earth and man. The namer is present and not present at once.

This naming of the unknowable God, this calling of the radical personal being by the name of God, is truly honest epistemology. Stanley L. Jaki reminds us that 'sound epistemology and satisfactory explanation of Genesis I are bound up with one another to a far greater degree than this may appear at first sight.'[1] The phrase by Descartes, 'I think, therefore I am,' is a distant echo of the honest epistemology of Genesis.

Adult cognition — and the distinction 'adult' is important to make — involves a direct confrontation with one's own thinking. This thinking unfolds in the house or habitation of personal being, that is, in the individual man or woman who thinks it. But *who* is this personal being? I did not name myself, I did not create myself. The more I try to find my 'personal being,' the more it disappears into a past of dependency, immaturity, and unformedness. I am but one link in a vast chain of generations. There is no certain beginning point where I began, all of a sudden, to 'think for myself.' Thinking is something gradually built up in me over time, after a long period of childhood, language-learning, experience, and education.

Genesis acknowledges this personal being as God. This acknowledgement is what is meant by the phrase, often emphasized in religion, of the 'human dependency upon God.' Religion can be faulted at times for not making the point in a philosophically honest manner. 'God-inflation' and false piety result when one overemphasizes the 'dependency upon God' to the point of human weakness and insignificance. But what I believe Genesis to be emphasizing is not so much human weakness and insignificance as the situation of human thinking and its limits.

Yet simultaneously with this acknowledgement of personal being as God, and with stunning brevity, Genesis says that the world — and therefore, thinking — has a beginning.

This world's — this thought's — beginning is not a chain of events, not a process, not a link in the chain of happenstance. It is *the beginning!* There is no 'before'; and where there is no 'before,' there can be no 'after.' For where there is *only* beginning, no before and no after, how can there be anything that is 'begun'? We are plunged into the stream of endless beginning. For if there is only beginning there is, logically, no beginning: there is only IS!

Thus the phrase, *in the beginning,* is radically *ontological. Ontos,* a term from Greek philosophy, means 'Being,' and an ontological statement says that something has being, it exists — that 'Something IS!' And all we know of this is-ness at the moment in Genesis is that it is allied with a personal being called

God. All we know, in fact, is that thought — this thought of the beginning — exists.

A rational philosopher might ask: Why something, not nothing? Thus he steps away from himself, outside of himself. By seeming obvious, the question appears modest. But why does any human being have the right to ask of the universe why it should exist? Thus 'Why something, not nothing?' is not a modest question. It is an arrogant question. Rationalism, by pretending to ask the obvious question, by sidestepping the fact of personal being, injects a dime's worth of false modesty into the thought process. At the end of the reasoning process, a mere dime's worth may culminate in a mountain of distortion.

The epistemological statement with which Genesis begins is uncompromisingly honest. It gives the name of personal being as God because no one can name himself and it says here is where the thought begins.

The question may be asked here: why one God and not many?

The existence of many gods is actually a more common, and maybe even a more evident, place for human speculation to begin when it confronts the question of how the world is the way it is and how it was made. This is called polytheism, and it is normally contrasted with the monotheism that characterizes the biblical heritage.

In my view, Genesis is first and foremost an epistemological document because it has to do with the appearance of thought. Cosmogony (how the world came to be the way it is) is secondary. St. Augustine took Genesis I for a true history of the making of the physical world.[2] The idea has persisted long. But this is too big a leap to make 'in the beginning.' Before we can understand what Genesis is saying about the creation of the world, we need to understand what it is saying about the appearance of thought. For, obviously, it is by means of thoughts that we discuss the creation of the world — as anything else.

Thought appears only by means of, by virtue of, thanks to, allied with, a unitary personal being. The God of Genesis is not an abstraction. It is a crystallization. For, even if there were many gods, to deal with thought, *in and of itself,* is to deal with how that thought appears in a unitary personal being. Yet in fact, the 'God'

who is named in this portion of the Creation story is given a plural name — about which more in a moment.

Indeed, the real imaginative exercise is not, Why something,
not nothing? but rather: Can thought exist otherwise than through
the vehicle of personal being? Is thought the unique manifestation
of personal being, or is it somehow objectively-existing and
spread through the cosmos?

If there are indeed many gods in the universe (which is a reasonable assumption for people to make) then we could assume
that there are many different kinds of thoughts in the universe.
There may be such thought-stuff in the universe, but it is not
the subject of Genesis. Because the subject of Genesis is not the
kinds and varieties of thought that may potentially exist in the
universe, but thought itself: the essence, the rock-bottom, the
absolute boundary and limit. Thought in its integrity resolves into
God. This is the proclamation of Genesis.

The Spanish philosopher Ortega y Gasset (1883–1955) once
commented that the assertion, 'Thought exists,' already contains
subject and predicate. Descartes had said, 'I think, therefore I
am,' and Ortega was commenting on this Cartesian *cogito*. Why,
'I am'? Or indeed, why 'I think'? Ortega's point was that the assertion 'Thought exists' is sufficient for us to know of the existence of a thinker. For we have no means of knowing whether
thought can come about in any way other than through a thinker,
a personal being.

Ortega went on to say that Descartes might have said, 'Thought
exists, as also the necessity of communicating it.' Thought, the
existence of a thought, presupposes the existence of a thinker.
Furthermore, thought presupposes communication. An uncommunicated thought is possible in the temporal sense ('I have a
thought but I am not yet ready or able to communicate it.' But
note, even there I am drawing attention to the existence of the
thought and communicating it in that sense.) Uncommunicated
thought can exist in the temporal world, but it seems to me an
impossibility in an ontological sense. That is, I cannot conceive of
the actual existence of uncommunicated thought. I cannot get my
mind around it. No matter how hard I try, I cannot picture to myself a thought lying around existing in and for itself, because

thought always has some bearing on one's own or other minds. And it even has a bearing on myself, for thought is that which enables me to have a relation with myself. That a thought could just lie there inactivated, incommunicado, is beyond my power to imagine.

That I cannot think a thought that is incommunicable is not to say that there are thoughts that are very complex, refined, elaborate, and difficult to express. The discipline of having and expressing thoughts is long and arduous, but again, it is one of those things that Genesis doesn't say because it is obvious. Whoever wrote Genesis — and its attribution to Moses biblical epistemology can accept — possessed a mind working at maximum pitch and tension. Intense brevity and majestic clarity are fruits of a mental effort and discipline of which it is difficult for modern men to conceive. More akin to music than anything resembling the intellectual thinking we know today, each thought in the Creation account is concretely stated and defined. Clear limits apply.

The Creation is the beginning of something — not a process, development, or emanation. The Creation account in Genesis is thus distinctly different from the Kabbalah, the mystical tradition in Judaism. In the 'Book of Creation' in the Kabbalistic tradition, the *Sefer Yesirah,* it is declared that 'God created the world in 32 secret paths of wisdom.'[3] Vatic mysticism — the proclamation of secret truths in elaborately disguised prophetic metaphors — is alien to Genesis. Genesis I is 'conspicuously void in mythical elements.'[4] The question of what is symbolical and what is real is not a question; it has not even yet been asked. Thought itself precedes the asking of any question. The Creation account in Genesis is thought revealing itself.

Genesis tells us that the thought exists, it has a beginning. Genesis communicates the thought in the only framework known in which thoughts are known to exist, that is, as allied with a personal being. The thought that Genesis expresses is philosophical and epistemological.

For the first line in Genesis says there is thought, that it is allied with the personal being who is called God; that it has a beginning; that it has a relation to the world (heaven and earth) as one of

creator to created; and finally, it communicates this message in
eight words (less in the original Hebrew.)

The physicist Dirac, I think it was, once remarked that a true
sign of scientific elegance is the brevity of the equation. The laws
of the physical universe could be written on a piece of paper the
size of an envelope. The same might be said of Genesis. In stun-
ningly concise language Genesis tells us the laws of the moral and
epistemological world. But it has taken us several thousand years
to work out the implications of the 'Genesis equation.'

The Names of God

The phrase that begins with 'In the beginning' is not an ordinary
way of saying 'is.' The author of Genesis seems to want to stress
the special nature of the kind of statement he is making. He is
calling attention to the 'is' as original act, not process. This original act which is expressed in the first line of Genesis is what is
meant by the term *creatio ex nihilo,* creation out of nothing. But
this Latinization of the concept is something of a leap.[5] The idea
that something can come from nothing goes against the common
sense of today as of yesteryear. That things have causes and prior
conditions is not in dispute. Biblical epistemology calls attention
to the fact that before anything is made — before we can *say* that
anything has been made — we must have a thought, the means or
wherewithal to make such a statement. The author of Genesis
seems to be calling attention to is the fact that every time we say
'is' we are starting something. The line thus links *is* and originality rather than creating something from nothing.

The connection between 'is' and originality is not easy to perceive, because our saying 'is' about things is a process that goes
on all through our lives. The world and its things come into being
for us gradually as we learn to navigate this ocean of *is,* and this
swimming and getting along in the world involves mutuality and
agreement with others.

It is a curious fact, and one that has long puzzled scholars, that
the God to whom this deed of Creation is attributed is spoken of

in the plural. The God of the beginning of Genesis is called *Elohim,* or 'the Elohim.' According to the Scofield Reference Bible, the word derives from *El = strength,* and *Alah = to swear, to bind oneself by an oath, so implying faithfulness.* This word is a uni-plural noun, perhaps like our *pride* of lions or *school* of fish. In any case, the plurality of Beings implied by this word, Elohim, does seem to point us in the direction of mutuality and common agreement, which I said was so prominent a feature of our little word, 'is.'

It is only later in the Creation account that this name for God, Elohim, changes into a different one — Yahweh, or Jehovah. This change-over occurs at the stage of the creation of man.

The fact that in the Creation account there are these two differ-ent names for God gave rise to a theory. The view was promoted for some time among biblical scholars that there were two differ-ent authors, or two or more schools of thought, for the Creation story. These different schools were named the 'elohistic' and the 'jahvist' schools.

More recent scholarship seems to be moving away from such a fragmentary view of Genesis. This is a good thing, for to read this story as written by different authors and lacking in coherent in-spiration, is to lose it altogether. And to lose the coherence of this story is to lose the sense of dynamic development in thinking and how this dynamic development plays out in history.

In the name-change from Elohim to Jehovah, we can perceive by analogy different phases of history-making. The 'elohistic' phase is analogous to periods in which a human community decides what is to be, what is. There is a kind of re-creating of the *is,* a sprouting of possibilities, a kind of radical uncertainty and unsettlement. It may involve discussion and debate; it may in-volve conflict. But whatever it is, something new is in the works.

It would be interesting to look at certain historical periods with this 'elohistic' perspective in mind. Perhaps the American Con-stitutional Convention of the 1770s was such a period; perhaps the convulsions in atomic physics in the 1930s were another. It is probably in the nature of the case that such periods, highly cre-ative as they are, are relatively short. As Ortega y Gasset once remarked, human beings cannot bear not knowing what they think about something. A situation of an unsettled 'is-ness' certainly leads to not knowing what one thinks about things! Hence such periods settle into a 'Jehovistic' or secondary phase, in which, on the basis of their common agreements, people live by the consequences of what they have decided and work out the results.

What Is Revelation?

Thus I argue that the statement, 'In the beginning God created heaven and earth' is a revelation, a revelation of the *is*.

The concept of revelation is central in biblical studies. The literary critic, George Steiner, once took some scholars to task for failing to deal with the essential question of revelation. He was reviewing a book, *The Harvard Literary Guide to the Bible,* and in his January 11, 1988, review in the *New Yorker* magazine, he commented that '... the plain question of divine revelation — of orders of imaginings and composition signally different from almost anything we have known since — must be posed, must be faced squarely and unflinchingly ...' Indeed, George Steiner thought that a book on the Bible which failed even to raise the issue of revelation was intellectually dishonest, even cowardly.

Both in those who would defend them, and in those who would ignore them, the truths of revelation have, in the twentieth century, ceased to speak for many. We no longer believe in them. Or if we believe in them, we no longer understand them. A kind of disease has overtaken our topmost boughs — our highest faculties. Inspired reason is perhaps rare in any age, but the twentieth century has abolished even the concept of it. And yet, the thirst for revelation remains great.

The novelist Walker Percy, who devoted many years of his life to the study of language and meaning, was very moved by the story of Helen Keller. This child — deaf, blind, and dumb, and more like a wild animal in certain respects than a human, was able to acquire language at the relatively late age of seven. Thanks to the devotion of her teacher, Anne Sullivan, who had worked tirelessly over a long period to spell out the letters of words in her hand, Helen had some preparation on that summer afternoon in Tuscumbia, Alabama, in 1887. As Miss Sullivan pulled the handle of the water-pump, spilling water over one of Helen's hands while quickly spelling 'water' in the other, Helen stood as if transfixed. She 'got' it at last: the revelation of the 'is,' the world of mutuality and common agreement, the world of symbolic connection, the human world, the language world.

Percy describes Helen Keller's revelation of the mystery of the 'Is' as the act of naming:

> Naming is unique in natural history because for the first time a being in the universe stands apart from the universe and affirms some other being to be what it is. In this act, for the first time, 'is' is spoken. What does this mean? If something important has happened, why can't we talk about it as we talk about everything else, in the familiar language of space-time events?[6]

We cannot speak of 'is' in the 'familiar language of space-time events,' because 'is' is that which enables us to enter the world of space and time. Genesis reveals this enabling 'is' to be allied with the personal being, God.

The message is difficult for modern man to swallow. The thrust toward personal autonomy which characterizes modern history to such a great degree has been at odds with the truths of revelation that depend upon God. The truths of revelation have also suffered in the hands of those who would defend them. These truths, having to do with thought and the 'is,' are instead held up as coercive objects of belief. The epistemological study of the Bible is the attempt to bring biblical revelation to the attention of modern man in a way that is neither coercive nor crippling.

Revelation:
The Metaphysical Status of an Original Act

At the most basic level, revelation must involve both original act and process. If it didn't have something in the nature of process about it, we would have no way of relating to it. If it were not an act, we would not be able to remember it. To ask about the metaphysical status of something is to ask what role that something plays in our lives. How important is it? What are its principles, antecedents, causes, characteristics, tendencies, assumptions, forces? What is its being, its nature?

The Oxford English Dictionary defines metaphysics as 'that branch of speculation which deals with first principles of things, including such concepts as being, substance, essence, time, space, cause, identity, etc.' The word derives from Greek philosophy: *meta,* meaning above or beyond + *physis,* nature. A metaphysical statement goes beyond what is immediately evident to the senses. *The Oxford Companion to the Mind* acknowledges that:

> ... It is a moot point how far science is, or can be, free of
> metaphysics. There may be untested and even forever
> untestable theoretical assumptions which are necessary for
> interpreting experiments. These assumptions are (by defi-
> nition) metaphysical, for they are not testable by observa-
> tion or experiment and so are essentially speculative.

The Bible does not have a metaphysics, at least not in the Greek sense — that is, not in the sense that has developed out of Greek philosophy and the rationalist tradition. If metaphysics *in some sense* is a requirement for knowledge in the rationalist tradition, the Bible does not have a metaphysics. If metaphysics is taken to be a requirement for knowledge that we nevertheless cannot prove or test, the Bible has no such requirement.

But there is a biblical requirement for knowledge. But it is in no way extrasensory or supernatural or 'speculative.' In the Bible, the act of knowing is bound up with the requirement for fruitfulness. When Genesis tells us that 'Adam knew his wife,' we understand that phrase to refer to an act of sexual union. The Hebrew word for knowledge, *yadha,* means 'union.' *Knowing* means uniting with, being fruitful, being productive, fertile. Even our word 'concept' carries the idea of 'conceiving' — a child or an idea.

Biblical commentators have made much of God's injunction to Adam and Eve to 'be fruitful and multiply.' This is commonly taken as an encouragement to fill the earth with their progeny. Physical procreation is indeed held up as an important task of men and women. In the epistemological reading of the Bible, however, we can take it a step further. In biblical epistemology, the requirement of fruitfulness becomes the requirement for thinking itself. It is *thinking* which must become fruitful.

Thus 'metaphysical status' of something, from the biblical perspective, must have something to do with the fruitfulness of an idea. Obviously, now that we have uncovered the idea of fruitfulness, we are dealing with an enormous new factor: that is to say, we are dealing with *time.* For fruitfulness is a time-process; or rather, it can only be determined when we take account of a passage of time — from conception, through gestation, to birth. The fruitfulness of something cannot be ascertained in the instant; we have to see if the idea we have had, the seed we have planted, will unfold.

In classical metaphysics 'time' is an idea that philosophical reason inquires into; it is a metaphysical idea; it is something that men can 'think about.' The Hebrew thinker, by contrast, does not place himself apart from time. Just as he perceives outward human life as a project unfolding in time, that is, historically, his inward life is rooted in time. For the Greek thinker, the *soul* was within. For the Hebrew thinker, *time* is within. This 'within-ness' of time is the essential thing to understand about biblical epistemology.

Thus fruitfulness is something that is a little bit different from truth. We can confirm almost instantaneously if someone who says 2 + 2 = 4 is telling the truth. We can also verify if something that happened actually did happen. Evidence, verification, demonstration, experiment, and so on — all of these take time, of

course. But this 'taking of time' does not inhere in truth itself.
Theoretically, through advanced computers and calculating ma-
chines, it would be possible to arrive at the truth of certain kinds
of statements (e.g. mathematical ones) almost instantaneously.

But fruitfulness makes us wait. We are in a different relationship to fruitfulness than we are with truth. We can be impatient to
get to the truth of something, and our impatience may hasten our
research and help us arrive at an answer more quickly than if we
had not been impatient. But all the impatience in the world will
not cause the seed to sprout before it is ready to do so or for the
word to be spoken before the speaker feels sufficient confidence
that his listener can receive it. In the biblical tradition, the question 'What is truth?' — spoken by Pontius Pilate to Jesus — is
met with silence. (John 19:38) It is not that the Hebrew tradition
cannot answer the question or that it refuses to do so. The context
and historical situation in which the question is asked have a bearing on the answer.

And why is this? Because 'substance,' that is, the content, the
thought, are features of reality that have a relation to time. For
even 'pure rationalism' lives in this within-ness of time, the essential aspect of reality, of everything that is. There can be no
'substance' apart from this reality. What does this do to our concept of 'substance' — of 'things,' of nature, of objectivity, of
'phenomena': of 'it-ness' in general? *It is that it is!* Yes, indeed,
and the Bible affirms this physical world. But the emphasis is on
the 'is' more than the 'it.'

May I say here that my contrast of truth and fruitfulness is not
intended to demean the noble idea of truth. I believe that truth, or
rather the search for truth, is essential, and that human beings demean themselves when they cease to struggle for it. Nevertheless,
I am only pointing out that truth can be dangerous. The danger of
truth is that it can lead to an abstraction from time. Truth, by not
seeming to demand the quality of patience from us, can itself be
demeaned. The biblical-epistemological reminder about the truth
of fruitfulness is an important corrective to this heedless propul-
sion into the realm of abstraction.

What is the truth of fruitfulness of the statement, 'In the beginning God created heaven and earth'? God is allied with the 'is,'

but not in an abstract way. That is to say, Being, the Is, is not an abstraction. It is involved in a time-process. The first evidence we have of this time-process is: heaven and earth. The sentence comes to a culmination with the words: heaven and earth. Heaven and earth are created. Something has been accomplished. In that sense it is 'past.' Nevertheless, it is with us still, and we have to take account of it.

Oddly enough, Greek metaphysics propels us into a realm of abstraction: time, space, identity, causation, etc. The Hebrew metaphysics grounds us in the world of real things: heaven and earth. Hebrew metaphysics says: *this is really here.* Something has happened that we need to take account of. But because it happened in the past, does that mean that it happens the same way now?

No. Look at the second half of the statement, *Revelation has to do with the metaphysical status (biblical) of an original act.* If the act of creating heaven and earth was an original act of 'is' when it happened, by definition an original act of 'is' could not be the same now. Many, many things have intervened since, things which we have to take account of. An original act of 'is' now is different. But being different does not mean it is less original. Originality characterizes the 'is' — wherever it is.

It goes without saying that the 'is' of heaven and earth is a reality of a different order than the statement, say: 'Today is the day for the recycle pick-up.' One is great, and one is trivial. Nevertheless, I think the principle is the same. If what I have said is basically correct — that originality characterizes the 'is' — the principle should be discernible at whatever level we are discussing.

What is a principle of thinking anyway? A principle: *in principio.* In the beginning. A principle of thought has to do with the originality of thought, that a thought returns to the beginning. Thus we have returned to the starting point. We have enunciated our first principle.

Genesis I and the First Commandment

Thou shalt have no other gods before me.   *Exod.20:3*

I am going to return in my next chapter to the discussion of 'is-ness' and originality. But before doing so, I wish to conclude this chapter by a brief side trip to Sinai.

The reader will remember that Moses arrived at the mount of Sinai, and it was there that he received the Ten Commandments.

Of these Ten Commandments, I wish to focus particularly upon the First. The First Commandment is the essence of monotheism: *'Thou shalt have no other gods before me.'* Some of us may not like it. It is narrow. It is intolerant. The God of the Old Testament is called, not without reason, a 'jealous' God.

But I would have my reader carefully consider this command-ment in the light of the foregoing, the first line in Genesis. At the very least we would have to admit that this Old Testament God is absolutely honest. For the demand of monotheism — 'Thou shalt have no other gods before me,' is implied by the statement, 'In the beginning God created heaven and earth.' There is an internal consistency from the statement in Genesis concerning creation to the statement of the First Commandment in Exodus.

For consider: the fruitfulness of thinking, of original act, is that which must be preserved and guaranteed. This God who creates and commands has placed his seal, his imprimatur, upon the orig-inal act: his 'jealousy' exists in order to defend this position at all costs. Indeed the very principle of monotheism is at stake. The Creator God can do no less than insist upon primacy, if this cre-ation is to have any real meaning.

This God will not offer a reason for his assertion of prece-dence. Nor does he justify it. How could reason or justification have anything to do with an original act? That would be to say that there was something prior to the original act, that it wasn't re-ally original: reason and justification preceded it. What a head game, what an endless spiral into rationalization! But what is the opposite danger? The mere assertion of primacy; primacy as an act of self-assertion and of power.

By what authority does God assert this power? For one thing, he can point to the fruits of his endeavours: namely, heaven and earth. This God as Creator can point to the fruits of his creation, which, although he has created them, have, by virtue of their being, also bound and limited him.

For what is the real meaning of the truth of fruitfulness? Fruitfulness is limitation — a self-chosen limitation. The seed the we have planted, the tree whose fruits we await to ripen, is not just any seed, any tree, but highly particular: *this* seed, *this* tree. It is thanks to this particularity that this supposedly jealous God can point to his creations and say that he has abided by his them, he has brought them into existence, he has bestowed a dignified being upon them. This God has demonstrated that he has submitted himself to the laws of his own creations. Why should he not then demand that we abide by ours? This God has every right to make this demand of us.

The First Commandment places a zone of protection around the original act, the act of saying 'is' — as if to say that this 'is' is always original, always 'first,' always of utmost concern to God. Participation in this 'is' is *our* creation. God's assertion of primacy is the demand for our participation.

To be sure, in terms of original act, in which our commonplace participation consists in our repetitions of the word 'is,' we cannot always be assured of the truth of something we say in the moment when we say it. Because of this, we often wonder whether we should really speak up and affirm something, whether to take a stand, whether we are being right to do so.

We can only know something to be true if the sequence of events that follows from our initial statement proves to be fruitful: that is, whether it becomes enacted. It melts into the stream of history — our personal history, or the larger history of our time — where it acts on us in turn, where we continually have to define ourselves in terms of it.

There is, inescapably, an historical dimension in any truthtelling. Truth is retrospective, retroactive. It is not that 'history' tells the truth (or disguises or determines the truth) as it is that we are ineluctably involved with history in any attempt to tell the truth.

In the New Testament, the words are spoken: Ye shall know a tree by its fruits. This process of determining the truth of something by judging its consequences is what I call biblical metaphysics. The 'metaphysical' Bible tells us that the way to know the truth of something is to discover and understand its subsequent history.

This is what we must do with all metaphysical beginning. The statement 'In the beginning God created heaven and earth' is a statement about metaphysical beginning (biblical). The statement, 'Thou shalt have no other gods before me' is the statement that demands our ongoing participation in this biblical metaphysical beginning.

But how to we travel from the first statement to the second? What is the intervening link? We must become introduced to ourselves. We must discover man — that is, humanity, human beings, the human race. In Genesis this 'man' is called Adam. It is accordingly to the discovery of Adam that we must turn in our next chapter.

Chapter Three

Who Was Adam?

And God said, let there be light ...
And God said, let there be a firmament ...
And God said, let the earth bring forth grass ...
And God said, let there be light in the firmament ...
And God said, let the waters bring forth abundantly ...
And God said, let the earth bring forth the living creature ...
And God said, let us make man in our image ...
                                        Gen.1:3–26

Living on the Hinge

Genesis I establishes the human relation with the personal being, God. That our own personal being hinges, hangs from, depends, on God, makes a metaphor of a door. The door swings back and forth, with humanity to one side, in the 'shadowed' portion.[1] A door, partially opened into the interior of a building, shows this shadow or darker side. But humanity is not, properly speaking, in the interior. The personal being that is God creates the thought that leads to the idea of interior and exterior. By the time of Exodus, God speaks His name: *I am that I am.* (Exod.3:14)[2] The Being who is interiority Himself has finally spoken His own name, and it is the word each human individual says when he refers to himself.

This 'link' or 'hinge' or dependency upon God brings us back to the first etymology of the word, 'religion,' discussed in the introduction: religion refers to the human being's link or bond with the divine world.

A link connects; it does not lock. Using this analogy, we may
remark that for human beings to be too sure of their relation with
God can be problematic. Fanatical religiosity — 'a lock on the
truth' — can lead to what Simone Weil once referred to as a 'totalitarian spirituality.' On the other hand, materialistic philosophy
deprives man of any connection with spirituality, and it can lead
to secular forms of totalitarian tyranny. There may not have been
as many secular as religious wars in history. But the toll of blood
exacted in modern secular warfare exceeds, probably greatly (taking account of proportional population changes) the numbers
slain in religious wars. It does not excuse the bloodshed brought
on by religious wars to admit that wars seem to litter the fabric of
human history no matter what religion is present or absent. Neither defenders nor opponents of religion can take much comfort
from the historical record.

Biblical epistemology should not depend upon religion. It
should be debated in the open forum of thought, reason, and
commonsense. But because biblical epistemology is, after all, allied with biblical religion, which teaches the Fall of Man, realism
about human nature is ineluctably present. As Chesterton once remarked, the teaching of original sin is the one Christian doctrine
which is empirically verifiable.

Given this realism, biblical epistemology can deliver some important reminders. It speaks with a very different voice from that
typically sounding from modern scientists, technocrats, bureau-
crats, and social planners. Biblical epistemology is an epistemology of limits. In contrast to the grandiose claims for human power
and control that sound across many modern disciplines, biblical
epistemology says that the arena of genuine human freedom may
be very, very small. But within this small compass biblical epistemology waits with every muscle tensed and every bow strung.
'Mine enemies do smite me hip and thigh; but I will arise and return their blows.' Biblical epistemology stands for human spiritual freedom.

And this is more than 'living life to the full.' It is living in history in the whole of life; or living in the whole of life through
history. The full course from Genesis to Revelation is humanity's to tread. To leave out anything, even the smallest jot and

tittle, is to forsake the vision of spiritual freedom. We are the beings who are to live out the history that has already been imagined.

Making Distinctions

Our relation to God, which can best be situated in the 'between' of moral imagination — neither too sure nor too unsure — gives us the personal integrity to make the distinctions that life is always demanding of us.

For making distinctions is often laborious and unpleasant. It calls for exercising judgment, being held accountable, being on the spot, and often being wrong.

The labour of making distinctions begins in childhood with the acquisition of language. It does not feel like a labour, but rather playfulness and eagerness characterize learning at this stage. This period in its critical phase culminates around the age of five or six, though the refinements of syntactical ability must be acquired before the age of twelve or thirteen. (Robert Bly mentions this in his book, *The Sibling Society,* in connection with the over-exposure to mass media which retards this development of syntactical refinement.)

The foundation for thinking ability is laid in adolescence, culminating in the college years. Ideally by this point the reasonably educated person should be able to read, understand, and express himself or herself verbally and in writing with clarity, accuracy, and perhaps even some flair. (I should add that my discussion pertains only to education in the humanities.)

Serious adult thinking is a training that begins after all of these basic conditions have been met. Aristotle once said something to the effect that humans reach their intellectual peak around the age of 51. This indicates a thirty-year effort involved in the task of learning how to think. Along the way, this thinking person needs to master the medium in which he expresses his thoughts in order to communicate them to others, so that others may find them of interest and value.

The road, indeed, is long. The importance of a lengthy education is acknowledged in the Bible where it says that Abraham was
in his ninety-ninth year when the Covenant was revealed to him.
Moses, having spent his first forty years in Egypt and the second
forty wandering around in the desert, was in his eighties when he
received the Ten Commandments.[3] The youthfulness of Jesus is a
biblical anomaly. This youthfulness, this newness, so integral a
part of his message, must have shocked his elders and acquain-
tances in the Temple. It was radically unsettling. And yet the
Bible finishes with the Revelation, attributed to St. John in his
ripe old age. The Bible, unlike Yeats' Byzantium, *is* a country of
old men.

Thus biblical epistemology represents a type of philosophical
orientation appropriate to the rapidly changing demographics
of modern western societies. The medical and technological
sciences have enabled vast numbers of persons to live to a ripe,
and often unfortunately burdensome, old age. How physical
longevity without corresponding cognitive development plays
itself out is one of those Faustian bargains that modern science is
famous for. Science and maths are activities in which young, and
sometimes even quite young, people can excel. But the philosophy of what to do with all of this time cannot be forthcoming
from them. Biblical epistemology is an occupation for geriatrics
and old age.

* * * *

Leon Kass explores the Creation story in the light of making distinctions. He says in his essay, 'Evolution and the Bible,' *(Commentary,* Nov. 1988) that:

> Creation ... is the bringing of order out of chaos largely
> through acts of separation, division, distinction ... The
> creation of the world, in accordance with these intelligible
> principles, proceeds through an act of intelligible speech.
> Creation through speech fits creation by separation, for
> speech implies the making and recognition of distinctions.

This is excellent: but it is important to remember that all distinction presupposes relation, and all relation likewise presupposes distinction.

Thinking involves distinction (division) and relation (connection). For example, when I distinguish that big brown animal out there in the field as a 'cow,' that beast with quiet eyes and fragrant breath, I am actually connecting it with 'cowness,' with all cows, with the general concept *cow*.

Now consider connection or relation. For I have just told you this animal is a *cow* —not a horse, not a donkey. In making the identification I have separated or distinguished this animal from all others.

Distinguishing, which means to pull out or separate, actually involves a joining-together. Relating, on the other hand, involves separating, distinguishing, a dividing-from.

The cognitive situation, a kind of exchange or cross-over between distinguishing and relating, finds a physical counterpart in the visual system of the human being. *The Oxford Companion to the Mind* devotes a long chapter to the human visual system, about how 'the axons from the nasal half of each retina ... cross over to the other side of the brain in the optic chiasma ... The crossing in the optic chiasma thus ultimately enables the retinal inputs relating to the two views of the same part of the visual world to be brought together.'[4]

In biblical epistemology the act of cognition correlates with the form of the human body. The radical suggestion of biblical epistemology is that *the whole human body is the way it is because of cognitive or epistemological demands*. In studying biblical epistemology we are not, therefore, confined to the brain. The brain is only the fortress; the troops are all over the territory. Biblical epistemology surveys the troops, maps the movements, coordinates the positions, checks the supply lines, and in general reports on the success or failure of the defence.

Adam in Paradise

Adam in Paradise! Is there any other way to read this story than mythological? Alas, however much we may want to bask in it, however much we may want to enjoy the warm air, refreshing breezes and invigorating smells of the Garden of Eden, we are not permitted to stay there very long. Unfortunately our time there is all too brief. And even within the time that was given, remarkably much was going on — or so it seems.

Adam's residence in Paradise is often interpreted as a period of grace — of bliss — a time of not having to work. This picture may do an injustice to the Paradise story. The story of Adam can provide guidance or orientation in thinking. For in trying to get to Adam, the bone, the skeleton, the reality of Adam, we have to keep in mind that we are trying to make our thinking fruitful. Adam in Paradise is a figure, a story, a myth, that leads us to ask about thinking, about what happens when we think.

A point of orientation for thinking is given early in the Creation story, prior to the creation of Adam. For example, shortly following the opening statement of Genesis, there are statements to the effect that God called the light into being, that he separated the light from the dark, and that he divided the waters above from the waters below. Distinctions are being made, things are called by name, they are set forth into independent existence. Here is a thinking act, so to speak, *rounding off* its experiences, its accomplishments. The world begins to be filled with 'Appearances,' with 'rounded' planets, stars, orbits, years, days, cycles of time. There is an indication of closure, of completion, of things returning to themselves.

Here is another characterization of appearances: *Appearances are the returning of things to themselves.*

Eternal Return is an idea which the philosopher Nietzsche made much of, and was a common feature of some Eastern philosophies. The perception of appearances, of things returning to themselves, lies at the basis of it. 'There is nothing new under the sun.' A kind of world-weariness can set in, a kind of psychological Ptolemaic astronomy, in which everything is composed of cycles and epicycles. For it is not possible, with Eternal Return, to arrive at a concept of metaphysical beginning, of original act.

In Genesis there is a line of development commencing with the announcement of 'In the beginning,' which continues on through the cosmic pageantry — the creation of circular and cyclical forms.

Still, the importance in Genesis given to the horizon line, the separation of the 'waters above' from the 'waters below,' is a firm point of orientation for thinking. The first separation, that of day from night, is more cyclical. The horizon, the distinction between what is on the earth from 'the firmament,' implies more distinctly a break, a place where thinking begins.

This beginning point or epistemological horizon is a necessity for the act of thinking where this act possesses the *requirement for fruitfulness.* Real thinking begins with metaphysical beginning, with the saying of the 'is,' and this is what the Creation story sets out to describe. Such a thinking may indeed be said to begin with one who is 'firm in his oaths.'

Genesis is a kind of 'tough love' of epistemology. Granted, in everyday life, when we stand and say 'is,' we have no way of knowing whether this is the right place to begin, whether our knowledge and information suffices, whether we ought to take a step back and begin there. We overlook the horizon line; we just keep projecting backward and backward. Infinite regress is seductive. Kierkegaard compared it to irony — 'the subjective freedom that at all times has in its power the possibility of a beginning and is not handicapped by earlier situations. There is something seductive about all beginnings, because the subject is still free, and this is the enjoyment the ironist craves.'[5] The horizon line in Genesis is the necessary conceptual counterpart to the idea of metaphysical beginning.

* * * *

'And God said, Let us make man in our image, after our
likeness: and let them have dominion over the fish of the
sea, and over the fowl of the air, and over the cattle,
and over all the earth ...
   So God created man in his own image, in the image
of God created he him: male and female created he
them.'   Gen. 1:26f

Thus man, the male and female or male-female, appears on the
stage of Creation on the Sixth Day. Can we make epistemological
sense of man's ambiguous gender status?

This is the first, or elohistic, phase of human creation. Man appears as male-and-female. In Genesis, the act of thinking always
has a concrete correlation or manifestation. What is the correlation here? I would suggest our epistemological analogy to be the
struggle, the give-and-take, between thinking and meaning, or,
more narrowly, between distinction and relation.

Obviously any formulation like this must suffer from oversim-
plification in the extreme. The distinction between thinking and
meaning cannot be pressed too far. For they are in many ways
much the same thing. Meaning — however we may try to define
it (and it is very difficult to define) — may tilt more in the direction of receptivity, thinking more in the direction of activity.[6]
Meaning sets the stage where the thought can be perceived; the
thought enacts the drama. Meaning lights up the circumstances,
thinking hews the path.

But even these metaphorical expressions seem a bit forced.
And yet the wrestling-match or interactive exchange between
thinking and meaning does provide an analogy to man's creation
in the elohistic phase (man as male and female, or male-female).
In this way human creation at this stage may be viewed *epistemologically.*

This phase of human creation is soon succeeded by another.
This is the phase of Adamic creation, Adam-as-man. Why does
the apparent equality of the two sexes in Gen.1:27 give way, in
Gen.2:7, to an apparent preference toward male development?
How can we understand this turn of affairs epistemologically?

The answer to this question will emerge in the following.

Male and Female

If we understand the distinguishing faculty as 'male,' and the faculty of relating as 'female,' the apparent precedence given to the male development in Genesis is an epistemological necessity. Obviously such characterizations have nothing to do with gender categories as we know them today, nor even much with human life as it is actually lived in the historical world. The thought world and cognitive capacity are common to all. But this common world originally springs from what, in Genesis, appears to be a partnership, a complementarity.

Once we hypothesize that in Genesis 'male' and 'female' can be taken to mean 'distinction' and 'relation,' a whole new dimension unfolds in the biblical story. Indeed, it begins to tell its story, not in the pictorial way in which we read it in the Bible, but in a way where certain consequences follow from certain premises. It begins to tell a story about human thinking and cognition in such a way as to elicit from us a feeling of wonder and admiration. For we cannot help but see that we too are caught up in the drama, of our relationship to the world and to our own thinking, that is the story of Genesis.

Biblical epistemology always wants to show how thinking becomes *real* and *fruitful*. There is always an implication or a manifestation in our real flesh for the cognitive act. In the male, the 'distinction-making faculty' becomes fruitful in the seed, which is creative distinction-making in the flesh. On the internal or cognitive level, however, the thinking capacity retains the relational or receptive quality.

This same observation applies to the female sphere. There is an *obvious* or a *physical* manifestation alongside the *hidden* or *cognitive* one. The 'relational' aspect of thinking becomes, in woman, physical capacity, that is, receptiveness, the ability to conceive. In the cognitive sphere, on the other hand, there is an impulse for 'separatism,' for breaking away. This is what the Bible brings before us in the story of the Temptation.

The cognitive act does not exist for its own sake. Cognition,

thinking, in the terms in which biblical epistemology would have
us understand it, always exists in dynamic counterpoise to the
body. The thinking capacity always correlates with something
real in the body or in the world.

When studying the account of man's creation in Genesis, we
observe a *downward* movement. From the 'image of God' in
man's first appearance (Gen.1:26) the narrative proceeds to the
nostrils (Gen.2:7) when man receives the 'breath of life.' Following this, there is a reference to Adam's 'naming the creatures'
(Gen.2:20) which suggests that the mouth and lungs, and the
apparatus of speaking, is being brought into play. Then there is
the reference to Adam's need for a helpmeet, and of his being put
into a 'deep sleep' (Gen.2:21) and the creation of Eve through
Adam's rib. Enough is suggested to portray a downward descent,
proceeding from the head to the chest, limbs, and abdominal
area.

This 'downward descent' is an incarnational picture of the act
of making distinctions. In any act of discovery about the world,
we must first make distinctions about the things that come into
our view. It is not that the 'female' or the relational is not present.
We are always relating our findings to our general notions and expectations. And yet this 'general notion' or expectation is not
called up, as it were from deep sleep, until the time comes to
make our assumptions explicit. The relational aspect of cognition
is always present in our researches, though it may be hidden for a
time. In the Genesis account the female is deeply and intimately
present. It is within.

Let us think about the ribs for a moment. It is approximately
at the rib cage, or perhaps just a little below it, that the centre
of gravity is reached. It is a nodal point between what is above
and what is below, the point of exchange between the force of
uprightness or buoyancy, and the force of gravity or stability.

For the sake of simplicity, let us identify the region of the ribs
as the umbilical region. This is perhaps not exact, but it is close
enough for the purpose. It is true that above this umbilical region
man possesses a body — a literal, physical body. And yet this
upper physical bodily environment, besides being just physical,
is also geared to a 'symbolical' reality. Eyes, ears, brain, vocal

apparatus, hands, etc. are also in a sense a 'symbolical' body. They are attuned to an environment of *meaning*.

At least, I think this reading is consonant with Genesis. The question arises: what is the task of thinking with respect to this 'symbolical' body? It is to *literalize* it — that is, to *articulate* it.

And this, in fact, is what we see. Adam's 'creation' is the unfolding (or 'downfolding') of his skeleton. Our word, 'articulation,' reflects this, because it refers not only to the distinct vocal sounds of speech but also the formation and distinction of the bone and skeletal system.

As this divine-human 'descent' proceeds, it encounters a problem at the umbilical region. If above this region the human being needs to deal with symbolism and meaning, below this region he needs to deal with what comes from the earth, the encounter with gravity and fact. But how does thinking deal with the literal — with the things 'out there' — the pull of gravity and sense-experience?

The human being must *symbolize* it; he must translate this experience into a meaning that he can 'walk around with,' so to speak, in his head.

Imagine the human person divided into two parts, the line of division at the waist. Above this line, we need to translate meaning into fact. Below this line, we need to translate fact into meaning.

Now return to Adam for a moment. He has just spoken the names of things, the names of the creatures which the Lord God has brought before him. The creatures, the things of the world, exist 'out there' in fact. Adam's naming of them is a kind of *listening* for them, for their names. It is pure receptivity. Adam listens for their names in light of the image of God in which he has been created, the breath of God which he breathes and in which the sound is carried, the curvature of his ear in which God has stamped the form of a trumpet. His thinking and naming are like breathing, coming in by the nostrils, travelling through his vocal apparatus and discharging itself in his chest.

But what, in the meantime — from the waist to the ground — is Adam's 'inclination' — his *Fall?* It is to confront what is literal, what exists out there *in fact* — and assimilate it by making it symbolical.

And yet, something intervenes in the time. Adam has been making distinctions, he has been naming things. Then the Lord God puts him into a 'deep sleep.' Adam is about to reach the point when he must relate what he has learned. He must call up from his 'within-ness' the power to translate experience and fact into symbol.

But how can he have access to his own within-ness? The female lives there. The female must emerge into the flesh and into the day, leaving that 'within-ness' open for human cognitive activity.

In the biblical account, the story of the Temptation and Fall takes place soon after. It is highly compressed. But to go back to the narrative, let us return to the moment when Adam was making distinctions and naming things. We may ask: what has happened, in the meantime, to the light, the air, the breath, the sound, and the trumpet? This assimilation of fact into meaning must all take place within the enclosure of a hard, round skull. It is an interior of interiors, a place where the senses shrink into nerves, electric discharge, decay. We do not know much, even today, about this interior, this cranial organ. But the contrast between the *sensed* world and the *symbolized* world was and is so stunning that even thousands of years later people are still talking about it. The great divide, the devastating rift, the other side: the experience becomes the preoccupation of religion, mythology, philosophy, poetry, history, and now the neurological sciences. We can't get over it and probably never will, not until the end of time.

Thus the Temptation : — *the tendency 'merely to symbolize.'*

This is where the Tempter steps into the picture. The Tempter characterizes the things of the world not as objects in their own right to be 'listened for,' but as objects to be had, to be swallowed, to be eaten. The objects flamed out before us, they dazzled, for they seemed to call up a lack in ourselves. In forsaking the relation to the objects by means of thought, attention, listening for, perceiving, waiting — we substituted desire, discovering in ourselves not only a kind of craving for experience but also the right to it. And this craving for experience *was* the next step. We did have the right to it in the sense there was nowhere else to go and no other right to be had. But had we not compromised our digestive organism of attention, the artful celeritous magic of Lucifer-Satan would never have been able to deceive us into believing that our self-consciousness and our thinking were the same thing. Thus, with the tasting and eating of the apple, we chose the bloat of self-consciousness over the crystalline formative process of our interior. We swallowed too much at once. We never learned to swallow too well. We became sensorially cannibalistic. The muscles of our mind went into automatic. In the language of the street, we blew it.

For what was swallowed up by us in this way was — not thinking, not perceiving — but our own 'vehicle' or 'instrument of attention.' Rather, we choked on it. We have always had a difficulty in 'swallowing' it.

For what distinguishes the human creature from any other is not his cognition so much as his interiority: or rather, his cognition as it bears upon, enlarges, stabilizes, his interiority. What distinguishes the human is the capacity for spontaneous attention, an attention not forced upon us by environmental necessity. The Fall of Man caused a crippling shudder to ripple through our organism of attention. A lightning streak or form of serpent? The words that come to mind: narrow, wavering, sudden, lasting, and mean.

Our 'coming out' into the world was simultaneously an abandonment of our interior cavern as a place of wonder, warmth, worship. The Stone Age cave paintings express some of the original wealth of that inner life, with animal pictures on the walls — great living forms which the imagination of the artist captured in paint. The earth had once 'swallowed us,' but when we walked out of the caves, we had to learn how to swallow for ourselves. We had to learn how to carry the crystalline formative process of our own interior within ourselves and preserve it in a world full of dangers, desires, needs, necessities, and threats. It never was simple. It is not simple to this day.

The Fall and Descartes

In this strange and suggestive descriptive poetry of the Fall of Man, the point I am driving at is this: God advocates union of knowledge with incarnation; Lucifer argues for separation of knowledge through representation.

When the world becomes 'representation' in this way, we are forever haunted by the question: how real is our thinking? It is a constant struggle to make real what we have learned, to make our learning and culture vital again. Indeed, when culture becomes mere 'representation' we must strive against it, we must oppose it. For we seem to have the fundamental need to *incarnate in our being* all that remains outside us as mere 'representation.' We strive to throw it off, to speak and to act again from the centre of understanding.

Where do the thoughts that foster the formation of our interior come from?

This question provides us with a letter of introduction to Cartesian philosophy. Why should we be concerned with Descartes (1596–1650) in a book on biblical epistemology? Because Descartes' *Discourse on the Method* is a kind of alternative Genesis — a Genesis of the modern world. Almost every modern philosophy, point of view, ideology or doctrine is traceable in some way or another to the influence of this lucid French mathematician-philosopher. To read Descartes is to descend into the bowels of the Modern Age — a strange image to use for a writer so lucid and so clear.

Let me review the story of Descartes. Sometime in his thirties, Descartes conceived a passion to know only what was absolutely and indubitably true. His 'method' was to subject everything to doubt. The one thing he found he could not doubt was that he himself was doing the doubting:

> ... I noticed that while I thus wished to think all things
> false, it was absolutely essential that the 'I' who thought
> this should be somewhat, and remarking that this truth, *'I*

think, therefore I am,' was so certain and so assured that all the most extravagant suppositions brought forward by the sceptics were incapable of shaking it, I came to the conclusion that I could receive it without scruple as the first principle of the Philosophy for which I was seeking.[7]

From his thought Descartes discovered certainty for his own being. But where did the thought come from? Descartes glides over this question. It is so self-evident to him that he is the originator of his thought, that this thought came from his own 'within-ness.' But the problem of being the originator of his thought, which in turn assures his of his own existence, was so great that Descartes made a valiant effort to explicate his own dependency. Yet the God on whom he depends, the God who certifies the accuracy of his own perceptions, the God who would not permit the Deceiver to exist (so different from Genesis!) is not a God who converses with him, a God who speaks with him. It is a distant, unreachable, theological God, whom Descartes characterizes as 'infinite, eternal, immutable, omniscient.' But even this omniscient God cannot solve the problem for Descartes, which is the assumption that the within-ness of his thought means that he created it.

The very 'within-ness' of my thought, which assures me of my existence in the Cartesian sense, should also account for the origin of the thought. But the more I look at this, the more problematical it seems. It is problematical for me to receive assurance of my existence from my thought if I am also the creator of my thought. To hold this view is to condemn me to a kind of autistic existence, cut off from the world and other people: knowing myself, verifying myself, being within myself, self-driven. This it seems to me is the great problem of Cartesian philosophy — a kind of unbroken subjectivism, a vicious circle. Indeed in many ways, though my powers of thought in Cartesian philosophy are great, and may be pure and unsullied, I feel that I am in a kind of prison.

The problem of subjectivism in Descartes' philosophy made it very difficult for him to say which judgments are true. He realizes that he has a difficulty explaining our how judgments can be

accurate if we are solely the originators of our thought. He says:
'... it is almost impossible that our judgments should be so excellent or solid as they should have been had we complete use of our reason since our birth.' Somewhat lamely, in the end, he argues that his judgments and perceptions must be true, because God would not deceive him

But this is childish. The God in Genesis does not promise us that our judgments will be accurate, that the world will be safe, that cognition will be easy. The world of Genesis is a cosmos, full of all kinds of beings. It is a world in which evil has entered, in which the ability to make distinctions is critical, in which the serpent of deception is gorgeously arrayed.

The refusal by Descartes to confront the problem of evil has haunted modern philosophy ever since. The evil that we refuse to cognize 'breaks out' in history. We have to confront evil historically.

We stand at the abyss of this epistemological problem of evil. But whatever the dimensions of this abyss, whatever the dimensions of this problem, it is vastly more complicated than the Cartesian 'subject' which thinks apart from the objects. That is Descartes' apple — the apple in his Paradise of reason that he gave us all to swallow, and which has had such fateful consequences for us.

The Epistemological Task of Childhood

There is something to remember about Adam and Eve in Paradise. They had no childhood. Adam and Eve were *created*. This is the metaphysical premise, and it puts forward as a result a particular epistemological task.

When we ask what Adam and Eve were doing in the first days of their creation — to the extent that we can even ask such a question non-mythologically — we must perceive them to be engaged with the *epistemological task of childhood*. That is, they were in process of transforming the biological instrument into a biographical reality.

In this sense only paradisal man *thinks for himself.* There was nothing inherited, no predisposition or prior determinations. We saw how Descartes imagines a similar epistemological situation: that of having 'complete use of [his] reason' since birth. Adam and Eve in Paradise is this epistemological imagination. But whereas the Cartesian imagination seems to lead into increasing abstraction, the biblical imagination is preoccupied, from the first, with the question: how is thinking real? The intention to emphasize the realness and importance of this thinking, its connection to the body and the world, is there from the first.

Thinking correlates with the skeleton in man. The difference between godly knowing and Luciferic knowing is the question of whether man's autonomy, his autonomous knowledge, has a *real basis or an imaginary one.* The disaster of Luciferic knowing was mitigated when man was expelled from the Garden of Eden. By this act of expulsion God assured that man's autonomy would have real-world consequences.

Human history can be interpreted as a transformed or metamorphosed skeleton. History is the 'body' of mankind. In studying the Creation story in Genesis, we are studying the 'articulation' of the body of this *Man* who is called *Adam.* Adam soon disappears into a mythical past. But the ever-presence of history, the history in which we are immersed, puts us back upon the trail of Adam's memory. In every act of historical awareness we reclaim a portion of the memory of Adam as our own.

This thought will become the basis of some of our further reflections.

Chapter Four

Getting Somewhere

Salt and Self-Expression

In this chapter, we are going to take a walk around the territory covered so far. For we have arrived at a pause, a bend in the road. The first three chapters were crowded with new ideas, crammed with provisions for the journey. I hope to take this chapter at a more leisurely pace, allowing plenty of time for digestion.

Modern society can be described from many points of view. The particular angle that interests me at the moment is the idea of rush, of hurry, of not having enough time even to digest our meals, much less our ideas. I hinted in a previous chapter that one of the reasons for this rush may be that time has not been taken into account in the rational philosophy that developed out of Greek metaphysics. Rather, it has been taken account of in an abstract way, as an abstract idea, but not in a way that is fundamentally consequential to the philosophy. Biblical epistemology presents a different approach. From the first we are immersed in time as a reality, and we have to take account of it.

One of the points I stressed was the act of saying 'is.' Every time we say 'is,' we are participating, we are adding our perspective to the stock of mutuality in the universe which, in the first place, we drew upon in saying 'is.' 'It's a joint-stock world in all its parts,' said Melville in *Moby Dick,* meaning that no person can learn to say 'is' in isolation.

Normally we take our day-to-day participation for granted. Nor do we think much about the character of the thoughts we are adding to the stock, unless we are trying to write a book, or something of the sort, in which case we have to descend into the laboratory of our own minds and life-experience and make the best of the tools we find there — good, bad, or indifferent.

Writing books today involves a dramatic self-confrontation. Perhaps it always has, but in the old world, the world of our great-grandparents and before, self-confrontation was more likely to come about through religious and moral exhortation. Every Sunday morning, and in many cases daily, one was apt to hear lessons explicating not only the biblical story, but how one participated in it through the development of one's moral character.

Religion as character-lesson is less present nowadays, at least in the sense of regular moral drills. And on the other hand, the preoccupation with character and personality seems to have grown. Books have become personal testimonials, especially the tell-all memoir. But even with fiction, personality obsesses us; plot, style, and setting seem secondary. We moderns may be more uncertain as to what constitutes good moral character than our ancestors were. But the publishing/media world brings before us a multitude of characters to study, a multitude only too willing to let themselves be studied.

These multitudes of self-revealers tell something about our historical situation. Such people may not be too aware of what the rage for self-confession tells about society at large. They only know they want their voice to be heard, their participation to be stamped with the ticket of 'I was here.' It is a form of historical awareness and validation. The substance of the communication matters less than the act of self-expression — and sometimes where this substance is concerned, the more outrageous, the better.

Thus we may note that the propensity to reveal oneself may indicate an increase in a form of historical consciousness, however inchoate it may be. And it can also mean that the act of communication is being confused with self-expression.

In actuality, communication — the realm of what Martin Buber called the 'I' and the 'Thou' — has little to do with self-expression. Or rather, it has to do with it, but by the time the I-Thou level is reached, the 'Self' has been thoroughly salted.

Interiority is salt-forming. Lot's wife looked back to the Self that she had been, and became immobilized, a pillar of salt. (Gen.19:26) Interiority, that is, the salt-forming process of thoughts living within us, is something that accompanies us through life. We have to learn how to 'ex-press' it from us (that is, draw or press it out) rather than express the self by means of it. Salt in the earth is detrimental to the soil. But the 'salt of the earth' which characterizes the thought-formed interiority can become beneficial to history. It is the communicative element, the medium of participation; it is the mineral that gives our historical life flavour, palatability, memorableness. Truly salt is the 'seasoning' in the sense of Ecclesiastes, 'To everything there is a season.' We express the salt by means of the self, not the self by means of the salt.

The Extraordinary Nature of the Ordinary

Philosophy deals with extraordinary dimensions of life — or rather, the unusual and extraordinary dimensions of what is usual and ordinary. Plato remarked that all philosophy begins with wonder — not wonder at marvels, miracles and extraordinary occurrences, but wonder at the ordinary, the extraordinary nature of the ordinary.

This philosophical enterprise, finding the extraordinary in the ordinary, also has a lot to do with what becomes ordinary for us. For example, when Descartes said, 'I think, therefore I am,' this was extraordinary at the time. But it has become commonplace for us. Ortega y Gasset once remarked that this Cartesian philosophy undergirds modern man's whole outlook. He says in his *Some Lessons in Metaphysics,* that the root assumption of the modern age is that our primary relationship with things comes through thinking about them, and therefore, things are what they are when we think them. And elsewhere: 'The modern believes that he can suppress realities and build the world to his liking in the name of an idea.'[1]

It explains why modern man is essentially a revolutionary —

why he feels he has the right to change the world. So, we don't like government? Let's overthrow it. We don't like the limiting facts of biology? Let's postpone death, extend childbearing years, genetically altar plants, clone animals ... etc. etc. *ad infinitum ad nauseam*. Even though, time after time, events have shown that when man attempts to change everything according to his own ideas, certain problems are solved but new problems arise. This does not seem to call a halt to the rationalistic ambition to control. People who voice their objections are considered to be Luddites, anti-progress, and thus dismissed as ineffectual.

Indeed they are ineffectual. For the philosophical ideas that have fostered this development have grown into the terrain of history. Only when a sufficient number of people feel the need for a new way of looking at man's relationship to his thinking and to his world, will such a technological stampede be slowed. At such a time it will seem bizarre that mankind should have striven so hard to put rational control over everything. Our age, too, will someday become an historical antiquity — a museum for things that have been tried and abandoned.

My point in all this is to say that philosophical enterprises have ordinary consequences. They have historical consequences. Because, as time passes, we become immersed in the conditions brought about by the influence of philosophical ideas (among other things) we tend to take our historical situation as 'given,' like a fact of nature.

The odd thing is, though, our historical situation is a 'given.' But it is not a fact of nature, or even like a fact of nature. This distinction is one which biblical epistemology explores and develops. This is what distinguishes biblical epistemology from rationalism in general — whose weakness as a whole has been that it has dealt with abstract and timeless concepts and has not been able to incorporate history into its thinking.[2]

Why is this? Biblical epistemology connects the thought-world with temporality. What does this mean? It means that there is something between man and world which cannot be limited to the Cartesian framework of mental versus substantial world, of subject and object. A relationship comes amidst the subject and object. Man has a historical relationship with the world. Man and world co-exist together in this relationship.

Am I saying that 'history' is the source of my thought? That when I have a thought whose appearance is a surprise to me, that 'history' is the cause — that it has come bubbling up from the cauldron of history?

I don't think this is what I am saying. At least I *hope* this is not what I am saying. But what I *am* saying is that man has a historical relationship with the world precisely because he has, at times, new thoughts. That is to say, original act (i.e., the new thought) presupposes historical continuity. This is not to say my thought 'comes from' history. Rather, it is to say that I can have a thought because history exists, because it is a reality.

If I were to say, 'my thought comes from history,' I would be repeating the problem that led to the Fall. We are always doing this, not with eating apples, but because most anything can function as that poisoned apple for us. I would be taking the concept, history, and trying to swallow it whole. At the same time I would be objectifying it, pulling it away from me, as if it existed on its own terms. No. What I am saying is that because history is a reality, because I am living in the midst of it, it has *metaphysical status* (biblical). How can I make history into an apple — objectify it, 'reify' it (that is, make it into *res,* things) when I am already living in it, understanding things the way I do because of historical existence?

On account of the reality of history, my relationship to the world has such-and-such a character. The idea that comes to me from I know not where, the idea that strikes me as being in some way remarkable, is remarkable precisely because it helps to illuminate some facet of my life in the world that has become a problem for me. It helps me make more sense of some aspect of my historical situation.

Determinism

The obsession with personality and character that flames up in the
tabloids, the news and publishing media and in the everyday gos-
sip about the lifestyles of the rich, the famous, and the criminal,
springs from a particular kind of soil. If enigmatic motives and
powerful, ungovernable impulses seem typical of those personal-
ities who fascinate the public today, the philosophical proving-
ground in which such public images flourish has been sown with
the seeds of anti-personality and determinism.

That there can be such a thing as 'original act' goes against the
grain of modern forms of determinism. Descartes argued the law
of the conservation of Motion; Leibniz argued the law of the conservation of Force; Kant argued the law of the conservation of
Substance.[3] A deterministic philosophy says there can be nothing
new in nature; every event following is only a transformation of
the preceding. An impersonal fate such as decreed by determinism is so much more oppressive than a destiny controlled by a
personal god or Fate, no matter how arbitrary such a god or Fate
may be. There is always the hope with the latter that there can be
a break in the chain.

Why does the modern philosophical tradition seem to favour
determinism and tyranny? This question would lead us far afield,
into the deep waters of history and political science. On the one
hand this philosophical tradition fosters autonomy and free inquiry on the part of individuals; on the other it tends toward sta-
tism, bureaucracies, and the politicization (rationalization) of all
areas of life. Truly it is not just the passions and prejudices of man
that have proven to be the wild card in human communities.
Rationalism, too, is something of a wild horse that modern societies are having to learn how to corral.

In the popular realm, ideas often seem to carry a deterministic
influence. The Idea of Progress, for example, is often taken deter-
ministically: that is, 'You can't stop progress.' When Progress
usually means is the conquest of another custom or 'unused' re-
source by a commercial transaction — an open parcel of land, a

relationship between persons. A paraphrase of the words of Jesus relating to the Sabbath — The Sabbath was made for man, not man for the Sabbath — seems apposite here: was commerce made for man, or man for commerce?

Freudian psychology can also be used, or some would say misused, in a deterministic way, with its preoccupation with the decisive character of the events in early childhood. But even Freud seems like an apostle of freedom compared with the pharmacological doctrines reigning in psychotherapy today, in which drugs replace the commitment to conversation and cognitive work inherent in the original analyst-patient relationship.

My point is that, almost everywhere we turn, behind the smiling mask of modern freedoms we find determinism in a multiplicity of forms. How is modern man to escape from these networks of thought that all seem intent upon entrapping him?

The broad way, the well-travelled highway, is simply to refuse to be concerned — to make a gesture of rejection, to refuse to think. But most of us would rather not be judged to be living a shallow and thoughtless life. We would prefer to be considered mistaken rather than stupid. It may be true, unfortunately, that determinism in philosophy breeds stupidity in people. But in order for us not to have to confront this unpleasant possibility, we have, in the modern world, come up with an ingenious solution. One has to admire the human capacity to come up with clever solutions to unpleasant problems. We have come up with a doctrine that serves perfectly to mask our stupidity. We believe in Universal Tolerance.

Universal Tolerance refuses to judge one idea better than another, one philosophy or religion or way of life better than another. Universal Tolerance disdains standards. There is a free market in ideas, so it is thought, in which ideas compete. People can pick and choose. Showing a clear preference is *de trop* — 'politically incorrect.'[3] People — and by extension, society — are not to foster one way of life at the expense of another.

But — 'barbarism is the absence of standards to which appeal can be made.'[4] And the reason that such a view is barbaric is because people no longer believe that ideas have the power to lift them out of their isolation, apart-ness, and solitude. Barbarism is

dispersal, separation — an obsessive 'me' or 'mine,' a retreat
from public interaction to private preoccupation. Barbarism is
non-participation.

Such a situation is a *de facto* triumph of determinism. That is
to say, the real reigning idea in this theory is deterministic philosophy. When all ideas are of equal value, none are of any particular value. Which is to say that ideas play no particular role in
helping man to live a better, fuller, and more honourable life. The
net effect of this situation is to remove ideas from the list of
human options, thereby placing all emphasis upon mere appetites.
Ideas, in so far as they exist, are simply a matter of taste. Since
there is no disputing another's taste, there can be no argument
about ideas. In this insidious way a whole cultural tradition having to do with the force of ideas is trivialized and made to seem
unimportant.

Indeed, the cultural tradition of dialogue, of 'I' and 'Thou'
intermingling in conversation, the stimulus of casual interaction
between people in public: all of this is harmed by the failure to affirm standards. For this reason, high standards indicate a vigorous
and interactive public life. Low standards, on the other hand, indicate that a retreat into privacy is occurring, and that people no
longer expect vital casual daily encounters. Since I do not expect
or seek such encounters, why should I care if numbers of my fel-
low-citizens are poorly educated, badly dressed, and ill-man-
nered? After all, they have their soccer games, I my symphony
concerts; and never the twain shall meet.

Thus determinism injects a poison into society that has an effect on the day-to-day quality of life. Universal Tolerance wears
the mask of democratic equality. But in reality it is far from democratic. It helps destroy a viable public life on which an effective
democracy depends.

So far I have been describing the broad way and the well-travelled path. Put in the most unflattering terms, I have been
describing the stagnant majority. For to fall into the clutches of
determinism is to fall into the ranks of non-participants.

What of the minority? For not everyone, of course, is going to
be content with so small a dose of intellectual substance in their
lives.

The modern minority of the intellectually awakened has also discovered an ingenious solution to the mediocrity of the age. They do not think that the cultural inheritance is trivial and to be disregarded. On the contrary, they love to argue, debate, and prove points, and they have found a way to do it without challenging the reigning doctrine of comfortable complacency. They have discovered how to put quotation marks around the cultural tradition. They have become ironists, deconstructionists, cultural commissars.

By putting quotation marks around the cultural tradition, the ironist makes a parody of it. As Roger Kimball writes:

> It is easy to get lost in the maze of competing barbarisms: deconstruction, structuralism, post-colonialism, and queer theory for breakfast, post-deconstructive cultural studies and Lacanian feminism for lunch. Who can say what will be served up for dinner? *(New Criterion, June 1997)*

The sciences have been free from the most part from the silliness and trivialization that has overtaken the humanities. That is because the sciences are still considered to be the essential tools for human progress. Because they are still considered essential, truth and error, rather than preference or taste, are still considered to be the defining modes of validation. Humanistic studies only support civilization. And of course, we moderns think that our civilization is indestructible, no matter what we do, no matter how little thought we give to the problem of its maintenance. Only when we awaken to the need to support civilization will we have a vital humanistic tradition again.

Walking in Knowledge

Biblical epistemology begins with the whole human being considered as a living form: the human being who possesses a skeleton, who walks upright on two legs, the human being who has hands. Neither evolutionary science nor the Bible fail to accord the precedence to the animal world which is their due. The animal and other kingdoms appear first. Nevertheless, in the Genesis account the implications of the upright posture in man are more rigorously followed out than anything we have had to date in evolutionary science. One of these days, and possibly not too long in the future, it will be discovered that the Bible is more rigorous in its 'evolutionary' approach than the science we call by that name today.

I suggest that the fact that human beings possess two legs and walk upon them can become a key to organizing knowledge in a different way.

The principle of two-leggedness suggests to us that human beings organize their views of the world in two primary ways. The fact that we need both legs to walk, and that the two-ness of the legs becomes, at the umbilical region, the singleness of the trunk, suggests an intimate and mutually diffusive connection between them — a connection not so easy to establish when discussing these two aspects is necessarily abstract and simplified.

One of man's legs can be called the genealogical or the developmental. The genealogical view of reality says that D derives from C which derives from B which derives from A. Or, that A is the father of B who is the father of C who is the father of D.

We are very familiar with the genealogical approach in the Bible. The Bible is indeed the great genealogical story. The importance of the line of inheritance is evident. It is an important factor in the Hebrews' sense of themselves and their mission; it is an important factor in the development of their historical consciousness; and indeed, it is a God-given duty.

Science, when it aspires to achieve prediction, is genealogical. If A happens, B will result. If A, B, C, happen, we can expect D, E, and F. We call it causation, cause and effect. The line of motion is usually from the present to the future, but it can also be used to speculate on past conditions: when we know of D, we can be assured of A, B, and C. When applied appropriately, genealogical reasoning is obviously a very useful tool for understanding the world.

But man also stands on another leg, and this leg I call metaphysical. With metaphysical truth, in order to understand it, man must participate in it. He must be able to reproduce that truth within himself, if only on a simple and primitive level. In this sense metaphysical truth is not a new but a fuller truth. What must become clearer is the meaning of this participation in the particular phase of the coexistence of thoughts and world in which he is — that is, its significance for man's historical situation.

With metaphysical truth, we must 'draw out' of our particular circumstances a present meaning from our inward reservoir, our 'within-ness.' With metaphysical truth man must re-define the origin, the 'originality' of the relation of thoughts and world, in such a way to be true to the world of his time — to all that meets up with him on his 'epistemological horizon.'

These two ways of looking at the world help illuminate one of those minor philosophical mysteries, mentioned by the English poet-philosopher Coleridge, when he said that everyone is either a Platonist or an Aristotelian. The Platonist is primarily metaphysical; the Aristotelian primarily genealogical. Coleridge himself was 'metaphysical' where Wordsworth, his friend and collaborator, was genealogical. Wordsworth is very concerned with the development of things, and subtitled his most important poem, *The Prelude* — *'The Growth of the Poet's Mind.'* Coleridge, on the other hand, especially in 'The Rime of the Ancient Mariner,' 'Kubla Khan,' and so on, seems haunted by the idea of origins, of primordial or archetypal imagery, the question of sin and redemption.

Likewise in the sciences. Marx and Darwin seem primarily 'genealogical' thinkers — but with heavy elements of metaphysics — whereas Freud (though heavily genealogical) and Nietzsche seem 'metaphysical.' They intend to initiate new ways of looking at history or the psyche or philosophy; they are after new 'original beginnings.'

With genealogy, the emphasis is upon the process. With metaphysics, the emphasis is upon the act.

* * * *

There are particular passages in the New Testament where the idea of walking in knowledge on the two legs, genealogical and metaphysical, can help illuminate a thorny problem. These passages concern the genealogies of Jesus, in which there are discrepancies in the accounts of the birth-narrative. These discrepancies begin to make sense when we read them as recapitulations of metaphysical and genealogical motifs.

The Gospel of Matthew begins: *The book of generation of Jesus Christ, the son of David, the son of Abraham. Abraham begat Isaac; and Isaac begat Jacob; and Jacob begat Judah and his brethren* ...

The Matthew genealogy emphasizes the line of Abraham, and this genealogy of Abraham concludes with: *Joseph, the husband of Mary, of whom was born Jesus.* (Matt.1:2-16)

The Gospel of Luke begins its genealogy in the third chapter, and it begins: *And Jesus himself began to be about thirty years of age, being (as was supposed) the son of Joseph, which was the son of Heli* ... and so on.

The Luke narrative begins with Jesus at the mature age of thirty and it goes backward in time all the way back to Adam: ... *Which was the son of Enos, which was the son of Seth, which was the son of Adam, which was the son of God.* (Luke 3:23–38)

Both of these genealogies pass through the line of King David, but the Matthew genealogy comes down through Solomon, the king, and the Luke genealogy comes down through Nathan, the priest. Both Solomon and Nathan were sons of King David.

The discrepancies in the genealogies have given rise to much creative speculation. In Catholic teaching the two genealogies are said to be that of Joseph and Mary respectively. Although the 'Mary' genealogy (Luke) plainly begins with the statement that 'Jesus, [is] ... the son of Joseph,' and thus does not tell us about Mary's genealogy, the Catholic teaching does express the insight that the male and female are the two streams of our *biological* heritage which, when raised into consciousness and memory, become our *biographical* inheritance.

But more than biology and biography, the 'two legs' of the metaphysical and the genealogical are useful here. Jesus's descent from Abraham in Matthew is may be interpreted as a purely genealogical descent. His descent from Adam in the Gospel of Luke is a kind of metaphysical genealogy.

The Abrahamic descent takes place in historical time, from a point in time-past to this point in time-present. It begins with Abraham and moves through the line of descendants to Jesus.

The Adamic descent, on the other hand, is trans-temporal: it takes place in 'original' time, which is the time in which we are metaphysically situated. It is the 'now' from which we move backward into a past which was 'then,' although this past has not 'passed' because it remains in the ever-present living memory of Adam. Thus the genealogy in Luke significantly begins with Jesus, not only a Jesus born and living, but a Jesus who had attained the age of thirty years. This age of thirty is significant because it is the first real milestone in generational life. In terms of esoteric cosmological studies, thirty years is the time it takes the planet Saturn to make a complete orbital revolution, and Saturn or Kronos is the god of memory. The Jewish Sabbath, on the Saturday, commemorates this 'saturnine' memory.

That the Luke genealogy begins with Jesus at the age of thirty has been obscured by the emphasis, in the birth-story, of the infant born in the stable, the shepherds in the fields, the angel of the Annunciation, and so on — the Christmas story. But in the - genealogy, Luke subtly shifts the emphasis to the adulthood of Jesus. There are, roughly, three generations every century. We make the step into another generation every thirty years. Perhaps we may understand the whole problem of man in one sense to lie in the fact that his reproductive organism matures in less than half the time than his memory. The onset of puberty in early adolescence contrasts greatly with the arrival into adulthood in the early thirties.

In Abrahamic time, we interpret history in the light of our purposes. It is not that history is always moving along consonant with our purposes, nevertheless, our purposes give us our direction, our focus, and our means of interpreting events. In Adamic time, on the other hand, history is always being made anew, for in Adamic time we are in the *now,* astraddle the event, looking forward and back at once. In biblical development, 'Adam' came long before Abraham. But in terms of how the course of events in history unfolds, 'Adamic time' rests in the bosom of Abraham, it has to be carried by Abrahamic time. What is new cannot be confined to any framework of purpose, yet it can only be understood

in the light of that framework. Purpose is the vehicle of our historical understanding, yet it can only incorporate the new retrospectively — after it has already happened, after it is no longer
new.[5]

Thus there is a gap, an opening, between purpose and the new.
In this gap is where (or rather, is when) Jesus appears. This Being
who is Jesus thus presses against the boundaries of history as we
know it. He is a trans-historical Being, the union of purpose and
the new.

This idea of Jesus as the 'surprise in time' is furthered immeasurably in the Gospel of John, which identifies Jesus as the
Logos. The Johannine genealogy is purely metaphysical. The
Word which refers to interiority, the word by which we refer to
our individual self, is in relation to the God who created the
world. This 'I' has descended from the personal being who created the world, but it has reached a point of completion, of maturation. This 'I' or Logos has brought something new into the
world. Its interiority has become historical consciousness. When
Jesus says: 'Before Abraham was, I AM'! (John 8:58) the phrase
profoundly shocked Jesus's listeners. 'Then they took up stones
to cast at him ...' (John 8:59) Why is this?

What is shocking in the statement is how the notion of historicity (even Abraham, too, lived at a point in time) can change
our view of God. Through historical development and maturation,
we are no longer so wholly dependent upon God. This thought,
even today, is alarming to many people. They have connected the
idea of relation with that of dependency. How it is possible to be
independent of God and still be in relation to him remains an
enigma.

Even the word *relation* partakes of this difficulty. *Relation,*
meaning 'describe, tell,' derives from the Latin *re + latum,* supine.
The word *latum* is a past participle of *tollere,* to lift up, bear. Even
in our narrative, our telling or 'relating' of something, there is
implied an effort, a lifting-up out of the supine dependency. To relate something we have to overcome our natural inertia.

In the saying, 'Before Abraham was, I am!' the Adamic time
pauses, as it were, in the lap of Abrahamic time but goes beyond
it. This is a reversal of the normal course of time in biblical think-

ing. It is not that biblical thinking did not have the concept of 'Adamic time' — of original act, metaphysical status, the now, the revelation of the 'is.' It does. And we have been discussing these concepts in this book. But in the Bible this 'Adamic time' only understands itself in the context of the Abrahamic time. Adamic time covenants with the individual, Abraham. Remove Abraham, put Abraham himself in the context of time, and what do you have? Time itself is opened up and revealed as an abyss. Do you still have a covenant? Do you still have a meaning for the purposeful genealogy of Abraham?

Thus it is not only that the 'two legs' of knowledge that appear in the New Testament help to explicate the reality of descent as it pertains to the life of Jesus. The 'metaphysical' and the 'genealogical' have not only merged to become the historical. The historical itself has become a problem of descent. The question of the generations has become, as it were, *revolutionary*. Human beings who up until now lived their history through the unfolding of generational life now perceive their generational life to be unfolding in historical time. A kind of seismic shift is going on beneath their feet.

Generational life, for human beings, is a dynamic exchange between the genealogical and the metaphysical. Every generation, in its search to get somewhere, to know something, must come to terms with its metaphysical heritage of the past. It must walk a certain distance, it must arrive at a new position with respect to this heritage, at which point it begins to devote itself to its own set of genealogical problems. It must decide what is worthy of being passed on to the next generation.

'Adam' stands at the beginning of this genealogical and metaphysical riddle. We will take, therefore, another chapter to look at Adam, this time from a more genealogical point of view.

Chapter Five

About the Biological Story

The Vocal Tract

Let us turn to the research of the biologist. This chapter will focus on the emergence of the human speech-and-language organization, the vocal tract, purely in terms of its *biological* foundations. This is the approach taken by Philip Lieberman in his book, *The Biology and Evolution of Language*. Although Lieberman is a Darwinian and writes in terms of the struggle for existence, his approach to language parallels the perspective in Genesis in certain respects. Most strikingly, in the descriptions of modern biology as well as in Genesis, the 'descending movement' of the biological events sets the stage for a being who can have a cognitive life — a biography.

The heart of the book comprises Lieberman's research into what distinguishes the supralaryngeal airway (i.e. throat or larynx passage) of the adult human being from that of human infants and animals. Only in the former can we speak of the 'vocal tract' proper: 'The "unique" supralaryngeal airways of anatomically modern *Homo Sapiens* evolved to enhance vocal communication.' (p.271) Human newborns retain what he calls the 'standard-plan supralaryngeal airway' until about the third month.

The standard plan airway is more like a straight tube, in contrast to the airway of adult humans, which is 'a torturous channel, the nasopharynx failing to reach the larynx and the air currents turning at two right angles.' (p. 281).

In newborns the ribs are almost at right angles to the spine, and the larynx is positioned high with respect to the base of the skull. These anatomical features facilitate simultaneous breathing and suckling. From about the third month the ribs begin a downward slant as the larynx begins its descent. Lieberman quotes Negus, the author of a standard reference work on the larynx:

> There is a gradual descent [of the larynx] through the embryo and foetus and child. The reason for this descent depends partly on the assumption of erect posture, with the head flexed on the spine, so as to bring the eyes into a line of vision parallel with the ground ... But this alone would not account for the position, since similar changes have occurred in the higher Apes without a corresponding descent of the larynx. The determining factor in Man is the recession of the jaws; there is no prognathous snout ... The tongue however retains the size it had in Apes ... and in consequence it is curved, occupying a position partly in the mouth and partly in the pharynx ... briefly stated the tongue has pushed the larynx to a low position, opposite the fourth, fifth, and sixth cervical vertebrae. (p.276)

This development in man occurs at the expense of purely vegetative functions such as breathing, swallowing, and chewing. In purely Darwinian terms, the speech organization of the adult human is something of an anomaly. The biological function is actually suppressed. Lieberman writes:

> The peculiar deficiencies of the adult human supralaryngeal airways with respect to swallowing have long been noted. We simply are not very well designed with respect to swallowing, and thousands of deaths occur each year when people asphyxiate because a piece of food lodges in the larynx ...

The deficiencies do not occur to the same degree with the standard-plan supra-laryngeal airway, which is also better adapted to breathing and chewing. (p. 271)

Finally, with respect to the role of the rib cage in speaking, Lieberman remarks:

> The anatomy of the human rib cage ... allows us to regulate subglottal air pressure during expiration by using our intercostal muscles to oppose the elastic recoil force of the lungs. These maneuvers ... structure the basic form of the breath-group. The breath-group as a phonetic event accounts for the ensemble of acoustic cues that speakers use to segment speech into sentences and elements of the phrase structure ...
> These acoustic events follow from the physiology of the larynx and the segmenting of speech into episodes of expiration ... (p. 121)

These observations from biology are useful in highlighting the importance of the speech-organization — an importance which, as we have seen, is also acknowledged in the Genesis account. We also note that both Lieberman and Negus discuss the recession of the jaws and the descent of the larynx as anomalous in terms of purely 'vegetative' function. Genesis connects the anomalous happenings with the emergence of the two sexes as physical beings — a suggestion which, for the modern biologist, is obviously a moot point.

But the modern biologist finds himself at a loss to explain the meaning of these events. Lieberman's conclusion — that the biological events plus the 'enhanced cognitive power of the hominid brain in the late *Homo erectus* stage probably yielded human language' — is unsatisfying.

I contend that the unsatisfactory nature of the conclusion springs not from the data, but from the framework in which the data are to be interpreted. Lieberman enunciates his interpretive framework in the introductory pages of his work as follows:

> There is a general 'mosaic' principle that appears to govern the process of evolution that is consistent with alletic variation. *We are put together in bits and pieces that evolved separately.* When we look at the genetic mechanisms that

govern the development of even simple anatomical systems
like the upper and lower jaws, it is apparent that the
development of the lower jaw, the mandible, is not keyed
to that of the upper jaw ... Though the upper and lower
jaws are functionally related when we use our teeth, there
is no master gene that evolved to control their form. (p.6;
italics mine.)

The 'bits and pieces' attitude — the 'mosaic' idea — may not
necessarily be in contradiction to biblical epistemology. 'Mosaic'
evolution was defined by Stephen Jay Gould in his *Phylogeny and
Ontogeny,* as the refuting of 'the notion of harmonious development by affirming that individual organs could have independent
phyletic histories despite evident correlation of parts within the
organism.' But the difficulty here is the use of the mosaic principle to account for facts which are admittedly biologically anomalous. Lieberman has just masterfully described the biology of the
human vocal tract, how it correlates with the recession of the
jaws, the upright posture, and the advanced power of the human
brain ... all to 'produce language'! This is quite a considerable
number of bits and pieces to evolve coherently![1]

It would be a great solution to the puzzle if we actually knew
how human beings once acquired language. Susanne K. Langer
brings the point home:

Language, though normally learned in infancy without any
compulsion or formal training, is none the less a product
of sheer learning, an art handed down from generation to
generation ... This throws us back upon an old and
mystifying problem. If we find no prototypes of speech in
the highest animals, and man will not even say the first
word by instinct, then how did all his tribes acquire their
various languages? Who began the art which we now all
have to learn? ... This problem is so baffling that it is no
longer considered respectable.[2]

Can We Look at the Fall of Man Biologically?

Our discussion of Genesis highlighted the significance of the umbilical region, the waist. It is remarkable that present-day scientists are calling attention to the muscles of the waist (the gluteus media) as a factor in human evolution. We share these muscles with the chimpanzees. In humans, they help prevent us from having too long a stride; in chimps they assist in climbing.

Genesis suggests that the umbilical region possesses not only biological significance, but also a moral one. The reader may recall the previous discussion in Chapter Three, in which we spoke of a 'descent of meaning' as the incarnational principle of the human form. But how is this principle to manifest in time? How will it reproduce? For remember, with Genesis we have an epistemological situation that needs to find a biological vehicle. Because modern science goes directly towards the biological facts, this pause at the threshold of an epistemological problem must seem very strange.

For Adam and Eve have no umbilicus; they are created beings. This is the epistemological premise that, for us, is so hard to accept. Yet to imagine such a situation is no odder than to imagine a hypothetically pure mathematical situation relating to physical concepts such as mass, acceleration, force, etc. Such began the road to exact science. The epistemological situation of Adam and Eve is akin to this 'mathematical purity,' but in a moral and cognitive sense. Adam and Eve's 'pure situation' dramatizes, with maximum intensity, the cognitive and moral dilemma in which we human beings find ourselves.

In the 'descent of meaning into fact,' and the 'ascent of fact into meaning' (these phrases being highly simplified, shorthand references to the human cognitive process) the midpoint or the line that has to be crossed, and again re-crossed, encircles the waist, the umbilical region. But the 'ascent of fact to meaning' does not make it all the way back, so to speak, on its return journey. Something has been left behind. In the cognitive return journey, the 'vitality' of the process becomes ensnared in the region of the reproductive organs.

These are simple, crude pictures for a situation that seems to be beyond imagining. Yet someday we may have to train our imagination in this way, closely focusing on the epistemological implications of the biological human form. Such research could have implications in fields of reproduction, ageing, memory, and learning. Someday we may find it necessary to supplement our scientific work in these realms with a research that comes from the depths of an interior understanding.

We may further note that in the discussion about the 'Fall of Man' in Chapter Three, we paid some attention to the act of swallowing. Philip Lieberman acknowledges that: 'We simply are not very well designed with respect to swallowing ...' Genesis connects the idea of a moral transgression with that of the act of eating and swallowing.

These two different ways of calling attention to an anomalous condition in the human vocal tract — what science calls a biological maladaptation and Genesis calls a moral fault — point to a potentially fruitful bridge-building between science and religion. We can correlate the moral or epistemological dimension with objective reality provided that:

  (1) it helps to illuminate already existing facts; or
  (2) it helps to fill in certain gaps in the existing explanation;
     or
  (3) it helps suggest new ways of building explanations or
     explanatory models.

But such a task cannot be fruitful until religion stops telling men to be good and science stops refusing to address the question of what the good is.[3]

Genesis compresses the biological events of human incarnation into the pictures of Creation, Temptation, and Fall. It makes the claim that human judgment was involved in human biology. On this point science has little to say.

Yet it is the factor of human moral agency — that is, human judgment — that has proved to be such a stumbling-block in modern evolutionary theory. Ideas such as natural selection have become a way we have of refusing to grant our distant ancestors any say in the process. Instead, we invoke the terms — evolution, natural selection, struggle for existence, chance variation, survival of the fittest, adaptation — as if in the hope that if one explanation will not do, perhaps another will. It is as much to say that our ancestors were all victims of impersonal forces.

It is hard to have it both ways. Either our forebears possessed moral agency from the beginning, and the decisions they made and the paths they took led to what we are today — or, they could not have been our ancestors in any meaningful (or precisely scientific) sense. Only metaphysically, that is, in the sense of the poetic and metaphysical idea of the Unity of Nature, are we related to them.

Indeed, it is to metaphysics that we must look when trying to penetrate the meaning of evolutionary theory. Gertrude Himmelfarb, in her *Darwin and the Darwinian Revolution,* acknowledged that: 'Some of the difficulties in Darwin's theory came from metaphysical confusion.' Even 'natural selection,' she said was a 'shorthand term' — a 'metaphor,' and Darwin admitted as much in the sixth edition of his *Origin of Species,* where he said that: 'in the literal sense of the word, no doubt, natural selection is a false term.'

But in human evolution, the metaphysics is already shouting at us. Mankind is the original problem. From the beginning this metaphysical problem is acknowledged in the Genesis account. There are two creations of man: the metaphysical one of the 'Image of God' creation of man as male-female (Elohim) and the genealogical one, of man created from the dust of the earth (Jehovah). Because the Bible is clear in its metaphysics, it can concentrate upon the genealogy. But in Darwinism, even valid genealogy is clouded by a metaphysics that will not announce itself openly.

Human Nature and Human Being

One of the puzzles of evolutionary theory is uncertainty concerning the difference (if there is one) between 'human nature' and 'human being.' Roger Lewin says:

> Exactly where brute nature ends ... and humanity begins is not a question for molecular or comparative biology. It is a question of the fourth dimension: a question of self-image. Here there are no lines accurately to be drawn, no hypotheses to be tested, for humanity's view of itself is constantly shifting, depending on the experience of the moment.[4]

This statement is, in a way, very odd. It could only have been written by late-twentieth century man, confused about what it means to be human. For the answer is very simple. Humanity has always been one generation removed from brute nature. In this sense 'evolution' is not a distant fact. Evolution happens every day. Being a parent and raising a child is evolution's daily grind.

Genesis wrestles with this fact that mankind is the 'original' problem. This man of 'mankind' could only come into physical manifestation once his thinking and volition met with conditions suitable for expression. This thinking and volition then undergo a developmental sequence so well described by modern biology, and, from a somewhat different perspective, by Genesis.

We may note that in the Genesis account that 'thinking' and 'volition' were united in the common task of bringing into physical incarnation the metaphysical reality. In theological language, Adam's will was God's will. Only with the eating from the Tree of Knowledge does man's will *separate,* that is, pursue a different direction from God's will. This is the standard theology of the Fall. We do not undermine it when we put on our epistemological spectacles and try to look at it more closely from that point of view.

The coming into bodily form of the human intelligence calls for an act of volition in thinking. The volition in thinking means making a commitment to the intelligible, to the principles of intelligibility. Language in large measure already makes this commitment for us. But the human being, himself or herself, has to make a gesture of consent or affirmation. This is an act of will, of positive action.

But self-achievement, self-articulation, the desire to realize oneself, the will to become, even commitment to the intelligible — all of these phrases have the pallor of tired platitudes, and can hardly express the 'breakthrough' to human being-ness which is indicated here. The historian Dilthey defined this breakthrough as the achievement of Experience, Expression, and Understanding. If we could understand how these crystallize, we could follow 'human nature' into 'human being.'[5]

Yet this breakthrough does not come about without cost. The world, as a result of this human achievement, becomes a known world, a world where thinking begins to follow well-worn tracks. In a manner of speaking, even thinking becomes a type of 'Appearance.' Only with great effort do human beings succeed in putting aside the mere appearance of thinking for the real thing, the crystallizing work on their interior. Humans have to persevere with their 'salt' for thinking to involve a dramatic encounter with God.

This struggle, in essence the statement of the problem of the Covenant, will be explored in a later chapter of this book.

Neoteny

In *The Biology and Evolution of Language* Philip Lieberman comes to another important conclusion. In the Preface to his book he says: 'The data I discuss in connection with the evolution of human speech again bear on the general question of the processes that were and are operant in human evolution — *these data refute the theory of neoteny.*' (Italics mine.)

The theory of neoteny states that the general form of man is an 'infantile,' that is, an unfinished or unspecialized form. Neoteny — 'holding onto youth' or 'staying back at a younger stage' —

was developed by Lewis Bolk in 1915 as the concept of *fetalization*. Bolk argued that in many respects the adult human is a primate fetus that has developed sexual maturity. In our time Stephen Jay Gould has, with some minor reservations, endorsed the theory of neoteny.[6]

The concept of neoteny is a striking idea which indicates the attempt, by modern man, to open up a path for dynamism in his thinking. For dynamism implies tension and polarity. The developmental aspect of man, i.e., the evolution, finds its polar counterpart in the idea of the 'unfinished,' undeveloped, or child-like form.

Where Philip Lieberman is concerned, I find myself contending once again not with his data but with his conclusions. I believe that his claim — that the adult human vocal tract is *not* a neotenous form, and that it cannot be understood biologically in terms of the theory of neoteny — to be absolutely correct.

But does the correctness of his conclusion in this sphere warrant the entire dismissal of the concept of neoteny? Here, as nowhere else, it is essential that we make a distinction between biological and cognitive process. If neoteny is that which shows what is biologically youthful in us, in our human form as a whole and in our life processes, would it not be possible to offer a contrasting principle, to illumine what is 'old' in us — or at the least what is biologically anomalous?

Thus we must place alongside the biological principle a *biographical* one: that which takes account of thinking and meaning. Only then will we be able to shake off the naturalistic bias of evolutionary theory. The reason that the cognitive apparatus is not a neotenous form is because *cognition itself is neoteny actually 'happening.' Incarnational thinking is the neotenizing principle in cognition.*

This idea came to Konrad Lorenz, who 'has persistently emphasized the persistently "juvenile" character of our behavioral flexibility ... [He argues] that "behavioral neoteny" is but another consequence of the developmental retardation ... "The constitutive character of man — the maintenance of active, creative interaction with the environment — is a neotenous phenomenon".'[7]

There is another very telling passage in Gould's book relating to neoteny. He remarks that:

> The correlation of maturation with loss of plasticity ... has long been recognized ... Haldane once facetiously suggested that Jesus be viewed as the prophet of human neoteny for his statement: 'Except ye be converted and become as little children, ye shall not enter the kingdom of heaven'. (Matt.18:3)

Yes, indeed! But why, 'facetiously'? The adverb 'facetiously' reveals the self-willed isolation of the scientist from the field of religious knowledge which, if approached in an open and philosophically attuned spirit, could further immeasurably the progress of his science.

The neotenizing Jesus! This is not an unworthy Jesus to stand behind the Son, the Saviour, the Prophet and the Teacher. Indeed, the 'neotenizing' principle is a key to the central dogma of the Christian faith: that is, the Incarnation of the Father into the Son.[8]

The biologist shows that the arising of the speech organization cannot be considered apart from the human form as a whole. The form of the human body makes possible the emergence of that kind of being who can have a cognitive life, a biography. So far and so much do Genesis and the modern biologist agree. But the biblical account takes cognizance of what the biological and skeletal events *mean for a biographical being.*

This is the dimension which, for modern man, is so startling. Modern man is not accustomed to having his meanings revealed, as it were, in so *inward* a fashion — in such a *participatory* fashion — a cosmic meaning, that is, *which we have participated in making.*

Darwin, Conquistador

Gertrude Himmelfarb has a revealing passage about Darwin,
oddly connecting Darwin to something Freud once said of
himself: 'Were it not so incongruous with his person,' she writes,
'it might be said of Darwin, as Freud once said of himself, "I am
not really a man of science, not an observer, not an experimenter,
and not a thinker. I am nothing but by temperament, a *conquistador* ... with the curiosity, the boldness, and the tenacity that belongs to that type of being".'[9]
A kind of confusion has been the legacy of Darwinian thought.
As Gertrude Himmelfarb put it, natural selection and evolution
and the host of other concepts seem to explain both everything
and nothing. We are left with hypotheses that can be 'bent into
any desired shape.'[10] There are many explanations vying for clarity; yet somehow the principle of clarity or intelligibility itself is
missing.
Confusion is an unfortunate legacy from the good, gentle, and
unassuming man that Darwin was — most unlike in personality
to the *conquistador,* as Himmelfarb admits. Though somewhat
culturally insensitive — Darwin's tastes were low, in music and
literature — he remained a man unspoiled by the fame that came
to him — industrious, unpretentious, a good husband and father.
The relation of a personality to the 'salt' of its thought is a mysterious one. There is something incongruous in the fact that a
gentle and unassuming nature should characterize the personality
of an individual whose thought crashed upon the world with the
tidal wave of modernity. Is there not something masked and terri-
fying about Darwin's very gentleness and unassumingness? Is not
this very gentle unassumingness something that we should fear?
— that we should be on our guard against?
The God of Judeo-Christianity is terrible, terrible in his
majesty! Because he is the God of mental clarity and liberty! He
is the God who attempts to warn and instruct his people, over and
over again, that there is no tyranny to be compared with the
tyranny of the gentle!

Chapter Six

My Brother's Keeper

Concept and Percept

Traditional biblical commentary, when it dealt with the Genesis story of the Fall of Man, approached the epistemological story from a moral point of view. Its sense for the 'originality' of the story centred upon the notion of sin. The concept of *original sin* has been central to biblical interpretation for nearly two millennia.

In this book the concept of original *act,* rather than original *sin,* has been emphasized. This is not to deny that the Creation story in Genesis is, in some fundamental way, a moral story — a story that tells how the world and human beings came to be the way they are and what this 'genesis' portends for our present and future possibilities. In this book, however, it is a moral story which we are trying to approach from an epistemological point of view.

The moral and the epistemological are both present in the story of Cain and Abel. This story has cast a long shadow in biblical studies. It seems that Adam and Eve had hardly been shown the door from Paradise when sorrows overtook them in the form of a conflict between their two sons. The slaying by the firstborn, Cain, of his second-born brother has been taken as an archetype, a paradigm situation of sibling rivalry. The Bible tells us that the reason Cain slew Abel was because God favoured Abel's sacrifice, and Cain was jealous. Yet Cain's cry when God confronts him — 'Am I my brother's keeper?' — remains the eternal question concerning the relation of one human being to another. The question burns itself into our minds as inescapable and maybe even unanswerable. For even God Himself, in the biblical account, does not answer it.

The fratricide, the slaying of Abel by Cain, is the first 'historical' deed of human beings after the expulsion from Paradise. This in itself is enough to call our attention to the story. But I think there is more than murder or morality which compels our interest. There is something within this tale of murder which asserts a claim to 'firstness,' to originality, and bids us pay close attention to it.

What bearing might this story have in terms of our epistemological Bible, the Bible that has to do with the act of thinking?

We have been asking questions about thinking in one form or another throughout this book. In the first chapter, for example, I characterized religious revelation as a way of paying attention to the act of thinking. Religious revelation does pay attention to the act of thinking, but indirectly. More directly, it communicates to our reason through symbolism and story-telling. This is certainly true of the story of Cain and Abel. The powerful symbolism of this story has obscured its epistemological focus.

In the theological tradition the story has often been read as the accompaniment to the Fall of Man — that is, the continuation of the Fall, the First Murder. In the theological reading, Cain has come in for some heavy condemnation. Possessive, jealous, impulsive, fratricidal: Cain's history is one of sorrow. In this reading Cain cries out for the Redeemer.

In esoteric circles, on the other hand, Cain has been all but rehabilitated. His special position as 'firstborn' from Paradise is emphasized: in his connection with the arts of metalworking and music; in his founding of cities; and in his descendants. In theology, passion, and spirituality, Cain is a towering figure, and overshadows his brother Abel, not only in the plot of the story, but also in its complex meaning.

Neither wholly hero nor wholly criminal, Cain in our epistemological study does illustrate the two-sided, double-edged nature of thinking when it is viewed in the light of the biblical, that is, moral, imagination. We can neither wholly approve nor wholly condemn Cain. Almost more than any other biblical story, the story of Cain and Abel makes us linger in the twilight of that moral imagination, where it is sometimes a little painful. It is easier, after all, to come down on one side or another. Holding two separate judgments and points of view at the same time about the central figure is difficult. That 'neoteny' we spoke of in the last chapter — that plasticity or elasticity of mental faculty — seems to be particularly called for in the story of Cain.

* * * *

'Thinking is an act of the soul whereby it becomes conscious of itself and of other things outside itself.' This elegant definition is from Christian Wolff (1679–1754), from his *Psychological Empirica,* and it is quoted by C.G. Jung in one of his essays. But finding a concise and useful definition of thinking is not easy. We are always thinking *about* things, but rarely do we think about the act of thinking itself. It often seems to be the case that thinking is 'the unobserved element in our ordinary mental and spiritual life.' (Rudolf Steiner)

For example, consider *The Oxford Companion to the Mind,* a reference book published in 1987 which contains all sorts of articles about the mind, consciousness, cognition. It is surprising, but true, that there is no entry under 'Thinking' as such, although there are two entries dealing with 'Thinkers, Independent,' and 'Thinking — How It Can Be Taught.' Rather remarkable, is it not — a book on cognition in the modern world in which everything is written *about* thinking except what thinking is itself?

In this same reference book there is a brief entry under 'epistemology,' the branch of philosophy concerned with the theory of knowledge. It says that much recent work in epistemology is concerned with distinguishing knowledge from belief — 'In what sense does the person who has knowledge differ from one who has a belief that may happen to be true?'

But once again, I must say that this question is not basic enough for our purpose. We have left Paradise, it is true. But now we have to discuss thinking in terms of the post-paradisal state, in terms of the story of Cain and Abel. We cannot begin to distinguish knowledge from belief until we define what knowledge is, and we cannot define what knowledge is until we explore further what thinking is.

So first let us look at the story. It begins:

> And Adam knew Eve his wife; and she conceived, and bare Cain, and said, I have gotten a man from the Lord. And she again bare his brother Abel. And Abel was a keeper of sheep, but Cain was a tiller of the ground. And in process of time it came to pass, that Cain brought of the fruit of the ground an offering unto the Lord. And Abel, he also brought the firstlings of the flock and of the fat thereof. And the Lord had respect unto Abel and to his offering. But unto Cain and to his offering he had not respect. And Cain was very wroth, and his countenance fell. (Gen.4:1–5).

'And Adam knew his wife.' We have discussed previously what this means. Knowledge in the Old Testament means an act of union. Conception is the product of knowledge as of the sexual act. To this day our language bears the traces of this connection: a pregnant wit, fertile imagination, brainchild, etc. A concept is something fruitful for us. We may not always be able to say what a concept is. It is not easy to define some concepts in words. An example sometimes given is the concept of riding a bicycle. In such a situation we are reduced to making gestures, making a pantomime of what bicycle riding involves.[1]

But after this tribute to knowledge and union in the biblical account, almost at once we are presented with a puzzling statement by Eve, when she says: *I have gotten a man from the Lord.*

Is Eve here taking pride in her reproductive capacity, as Leon and Amy Kass argue in their essay, 'What's Your Name?' *(First Things,* November, 1995) The Kasses remark as follows: 'Eve proudly boasts of her creative power in the birth of Cain ... the context, in our view, favours this meaning: "God created a man, and now so have I".'

With due respect to the Kasses, this interpretation seems to me a cumbersome projection of modern sentiments upon an inspired text. Considering the severe chastisement that has just followed the act of self-assertion — the eating from the Tree of Knowledge and the expulsion from Paradise — it seems farfetched to accuse Eve of prideful boasting.

Furthermore: boasting is a kind of deformation of the act of thinking. That is, when we boast about something we have done, it is because we are comparing our action to some other possible action. The boasting may be a false judgment, but it is a judgment. It presupposes the ability to discern difference and likeness, to engage in comparisons, to make distinctions. These are really quite subtle acts of intellect.

We need to find out first how intellect itself arises, before we can point to instances of how it is used (or misused.) And I contend that with the birth of Cain we have a picture of the birth of the intellect itself: more precisely, the birth of the *concept,* of *conceptual thinking.*

The name, 'Cain,' offers support to this interpretation. The Kasses give the meaning of the name, Cain, as deriving from a root meaning 'to possess.' A better synonym for our purpose, however, would be 'to acquire.' *Acquisition* and *possession* are very close in meaning. But 'possession' implies more of a material possession, that is the possession of material things, or perhaps a kind of unfulfillment in the soul — 'possessiveness.' This is true of Cain; he becomes possessive; he becomes jealous. But I will argue that the other meaning, acquirement, also applies to Cain. In the eighteenth century *acquirements* referred to learning, to the acquirements of knowledge. I believe that 'Cain' also signifies 'acquirement' in this sense.

Conceptual knowledge is added or *acquired.* 'Concepts cannot be gained through observation. This follows from the simple fact that the growing human being only slowly and gradually forms the concepts corresponding to the objects which surround him. Concepts are *added* to observation.'[2] How this adding or acquiring of concepts is accomplished in the growing human being comprises many elements of education, trial and error, life experience, language and memory.

But let us return to the story, especially to Eve's mysterious phrase, 'I have gotten a man of the Lord.' Emil Bock, a theologian, says that:

> The birth of Cain is hidden in a veil of greatest secrets. After Eve has given birth to her first son, Genesis has her saying the darkly mysterious words, 'As husband I have gained Yahweh'.[3]

Thus Bock's translation gives a slightly different sense to the words, one far removed from the 'prideful boasting' that the Kasses claimed to find in Eve's words.

Eve's statement — 'I have gotten a man from the Lord' or, 'As husband I have gained Jehovah' — begins to make sense when we see it as saying something important about the cognitive act. The divine power is experienced through the act of union: on the physical level it produces a child; on the cognitive level it produces knowledge; it indicates our participation. This divine power or 'participation in Being' is called, by Eve, 'gaining Jehovah' — getting a man from the Lord.

Eve's words, then, may signify her participant-understanding in the act of thinking. Eve's conceiving of Cain seems to hearken back to the time in Paradise when Adam 'named the beasts,' when human naming and speaking were defining, distinguishing forces. Eve, who has been named the 'mother of all living,' participates in gaining (the relation with) Jehovah through her conceiving. Her conceiving a child is no more just physical than Adam's conversational relation to the beings and creatures of the world was just cognitive. A unified physical and spiritual conception underlies both stories.

Eve's words, then, signify her realization of the participatory element underlying physical as of spiritual conception.[4] The words of the poet Francis Thompson may apply to Eve's experience of motherhood: 'My soul remembers its lost paradise.'

Likewise, the first-born Cain feels very strongly the connection with that earlier or paradisal part of human nature. For the capacity of speaking, relating, distinguishing, has been carried over from Paradise. But now it takes the form of conceptual thinking.

This new form of human capacity appears for the first time in Cain. Cain embodies it.

Cain is the farmer; he is the one who brings the plant offering, the bloodless offering. Why should he not but feel shock when he learns that the bloodless offering now no longer suffices? For this new capacity of conceptual thinking has entered the blood. The plant foods sufficed in Paradise. But things have changed since Paradise. There must be a new offering. 'Cain's gifts correspond to an already bygone aeon. They are no longer in keeping with the age.'[5]

Cain's shock gives an accurate picture of how we experience historical change. For it is not only that our ideas and world-view change with time. The whole world changes; the world we experience itself embodies this change. The world we grew up in no longer exists; our talents and expectations, by the time we achieve maturity, already seem disjunct and off-key to the world in which we are immersed. Thus there is not, strictly speaking, in the historical process that 'correlation between consciousness and nature' that characterizes the evolution of consciousness in general that Barfield spoke of.[6] The historical process is one of successive embodiment of evolving world views, customs, expectations, and thoughts. The correlative is thrown off-key. Very often it happens that individuals feel that they have been born out of their time, in the wrong time. Their talents do not quite fit the requirements of their age. Cain is one of these people.

Let us now turn to Abel — 'exhalation,' or 'breath that vanishes' (the Kasses) or 'that which ascends' (Emil Bock).

We do not only gain knowledge by means of concepts. *The Oxford Companion to the Mind* expends a long essay on Perception, about which, they remark, 'philosophers have a heavy investment.' Through perception, they write, 'our senses probe the external world.' Continuing:

> It is worth asking why we have both *perceptions* and
> *conceptions* of the world. Why is perception somehow
> separate, and in several ways different, from our
> conceptual understanding? Very likely it is because

> perception, in order to be useful, must work very quickly,
> whereas we may take years forming concepts, since
> knowledge and ideas are in a sense timeless ...

That timelessness, indeed, belongs to the conceptual world, the Cain-world. For example, we discussed previously how Greek metaphysical concepts were in a sense timeless — space, identity, causation, and the like. We spend years learning to assimilate such abstract concepts, and skill in using them is a lifelong task. Once we gain this skill, we are not likely to recall the lifelong effort involved in gaining it.

But, to continue, again from the same essay on Perception:

> It has usually been thought that perception occurs
> *passively* from inputs from the senses. It is now, however,
> fairly generally accepted that stored knowledge and
> assumptions *actively* affect even the simplest perceptions.[7]

Let us further consider the fate of perception, or the percept, in thinking.[8] A good example of the difference between a concept and a percept occurs in a case-study by Dr Oliver Sacks, the noted neurological physician. Dr Sacks had a patient, a Dr P., who suffered from 'visual agnosia,' i.e., the inability to conceptualize visual data.

Dr Sacks handed a rose to Dr P. and asked him to identify it. Dr P. took it in his hand and commented, 'About six inches in length ... a convoluted red form with a linear green attachment.'[9]

Dr P. was able to function perceptually — and on a quite abstract level. But he was unable to grasp the concept *rose* through his unaided visual sense.[10] And yet — how rich with poetic suggestiveness is his perceiving! We must admit, that while we often admire roses, that Dr P's 'convoluted red form with linear green attachment' makes us stop and appreciate the rose all over again from his perspective.

Dr P.'s perspective jolts us, and makes us become aware of something which, in the process of conceptualizing, has become *unconscious* — something which has undergone a 'little death.' What is it?

It is the very individuality and uniqueness of a thing which is subsumed in the conceptualizing faculty. And this, I think, is the real key to the Cain and Abel story. It is Abel's fate to be subsumed, to be slain, by his brother. Abel is 'the normal man of his time'[11] whose very 'normality' reveals the very freshness and particularity of things which is 'exhaled' in conceptualizing. The 'breath that vanishes' is *particularity itself,* absorbed into the general notions of our concepts.

The Destiny of Cain

A person may look at a phenomenon: which act implies in some sense a vow of faithfulness to *what is.* Or, a person may *think* that he is looking at something, whereas he is actually looking at himself look at something. Something has gotten interposed between himself and the world. He becomes enmeshed in his own toils rather than in what the world can say to him; he becomes exiled from the world. Does he not take on the destiny of Cain? — *I shall be a fugitive and a vagabond upon the earth.* (Gen.4:14)

Genesis recognizes this, but adds: *And the Lord said unto Cain, Therefore whosoever slayeth Cain, vengeance shall be taken on him sevenfold. And the Lord set a mark upon Cain, lest any finding him should kill him.* (Gen. 4:15)

For thinking cannot do otherwise than what it does in this story. We cannot have the capacity to form concepts — thus connecting with the realm of timeless generality — without the loss of the other — freshness and particularity. The Bible recognizes this moral ambiguity. God condemns, yet protects, Cain. Was the 'mark of Cain' a mark upon his *brow* — as if to underscore the seat of thinking? Thus the mark of Cain is not only his badge of shame; it is also the sign of the special protection accorded to him.

What would it mean to accept the moral imperative of being our brother's keeper with respect to the act of cognition? It would show us the necessity for a morally-responsible thinking, even for

an *act of recollection in thinking* — for remembering what happens every time we say that 'something is ...' We would become
aware of just how much loveliness and particularity has been
spilled in our brother's blood that crieth out to us from the
ground.

Chapter Seven

The Covenant

*For it was not the angels that he took to himself; he
took to himself the line of Abraham.*   Heb.2:16

Human Life in Effective Motion

The modern epistemologist asks how a person's knowledge
differs from a belief that happens to be true. Asking such a question is after all something that epistemologists are supposed to
do. Such a question, which would probably not occur to anyone
else, is asked on the far reaches of life, outside the hubbub of
dailiness and the demands of decision making. For most of us
have to take the knowledge we already have into the arena of our
life and work with that. We don't have the time to be always test-
ing and probing it beforehand, pricking it with theoretical questions and sticking thermometers in to check for vital signs. What
we have learned so far is what we have to go on, and our suc-
cesses, excesses, and shipwrecks add to our general store of
knowledge. It is called the school of experience.

This kind of knowledge we have for daily life is a special kind
of 'how-to' knowledge. Epistemology is more apt to ask, How do
I know what I know? rather than, How do I take apart the engine
of this car? Even if the car breaks down and they are at a loss to
proceed, having no mechanical knowledge, epistemologists do
not normally perceive human life on the same spectrum as a
mechanical breakdown and they often appear to be furiously
going through the motions of driving although the car is station-
ary. Scientists, on the other hand, still often continue to perceive

human life in terms of a mechanical model. They continue to beat this model with a stick, as if it were a mule, rather than inquiring into the fuel requirements for a human life in effective motion. This polarization of knowledge into two branches, theory and practice, is characteristic of our classical, philosophical and rational heritage. Theoretical knowledge is very refined and abstract and leads to the asking of questions that no one but a philosopher would think of asking, such as 'Was it within God's power to create any possible world he pleased?'[1] Alvin Plantinga says this question is 'crucial for the Free Will defence,' though how this should be so is, for the non-philosopher, difficult to see. For the non-philosopher, the world that we live in, the real world, the historical world, already presents such an overwhelming challenge that the question of other possible worlds seems to be a kind of dizzying superfluousness, a form of intellectual obesity.

Mechanical or practical knowledge, on the other hand, describes human life in terms of the automotive analogy, and it does so to perfection. It leaves nothing out except the question of who is driving the vehicle, and where. As Thoreau remarked of the railroad, the mechanical explanation is 'an improved means to an unimproved end.'

But if human life is indeed a car going somewhere, there ought to be laws of its construction, operation, and motion. And furthermore, there should be as many different ways of asking the question about this car going somewhere as there are of cooking a chicken. For instance, if the important part of the question is the 'going somewhere' rather than the 'car,' then we would have to admit that there are circumstances in which getting there on foot might be preferable to driving. And if the important part of the phrase is the 'somewhere' rather than the 'going,' we can start asking questions about the where and the why. There are all sorts of ways of asking questions without getting sidetracked into other possible worlds that God may have or may not have wanted to invent.

Biblical epistemology begins the asking of questions with the car going somewhere, not with the question, What is it anyway? We already know what it is; thinking is already harnessed to the world as-it-is. 'The aim of creation is history,' said Karl Barth, in one brief epigram summarizing many lengthy pages of his *Church Dogmatics.* The fact that the aim of creation is history takes a great weight off the shoulders of the epistemologist. His task is not so much to say what thinking is but how it works and what it is supposed to do. The epistemologist's job is to clear the intersection between thinking and actuality instead of making endless detours around it.

The history of rational thinking shows that the direct encounter of thinking with actuality — the pause at the intersection of creation and history — is not something that philosophers do particularly well. The existentialist and anti-metaphysical tendency in modern philosophy is in large part a reaction against the piling-up of barriers and blockades at the intersection. Whether the car is will or representation, or whether it might be a civilization-induced illusion; whether driving might be the thesis of personality or the antithesis of walking or just merely the synthesis of motion; whether moving is the thing-in-itself, or whether we just appear to move because that is how moving is translated by our minds; whether the rules of the road are eternal laws, or whether they are just culturally conditioned signals; whether there is an intersection ... whether there is a driver ... whether there is a there ... No wonder Karl Marx, in a fit of exasperation, declared that 'The philosophers have only *interpreted* the world, in various ways; the point, however, is to change it.' But even Marx's car crashed at the intersection. He might have said, with brilliant truth, that it was not religion, but philosophy, that was the opiate of the people.[2]

How does the Bible describe the encounter of thinking with actuality?

Voluntary Constraint

Genesis teaches us that God's command to Adam and Eve not to eat of the fruit of the tree of the knowledge of good and evil was a prohibition. It was the absolute *No!* — Thou shalt not. It was the forbidden, *verboten.* But even this absolute *verboten* was qualified by an *If:* if you eat of this tree, you will die. '... of the tree of the knowledge of good and evil, thou shalt not eat of it: for in the day that thou eatest thereof thou shalt surely die.' (Gen.2:17)

In a similar way to the parent who tells his child not to touch a hot stove, and who then modifies the prohibition with the reason, 'because it will burn you,' God forbids Adam and Eve from eating of the tree of knowledge 'because it will kill you.' The reason given is an afterthought, an idea without experiential content, since it can be assumed that the child has no prior experience of being burned, as Adam and Eve have no prior experience of death.

But what, really, is this 'reasonable afterthought'? Is it not a form of propositional knowledge: that is, knowledge which compels by its self-evident truth? If you eat of the tree of knowledge, you will die. If you touch a hot stove, you will be burned. If two and two are added together, they make four.

Knowledge in this form leaves us no choice. This kind of knowledge subjects us to a compulsion, in and of itself, that has nothing whatsoever to do with our own will, or indeed the will of any other. It is not that reasonable or rational truth 'expels' the personal will from the universe so much as the fact that it appears to have nothing whatsoever to do with the will. God's prohibition, on the other hand, makes an insistent claim that the will of God comes first in the world. It asserts that what is important is the relation, the relationship, between God and man, because God insists upon it. The important thing is that human beings maintain their relationship with the Creator. A rational and compelling knowledge intervenes between the Creator and the created.

Rationality — self-evident or compelling truth — leads away from the relation with God. God's prohibition is the assertion that the truth abides in the relation, not in the contents of 'reason.' As Lev Shestov puts it:

> ... all the commentators believed that the sin of the first man consisted in an act of disobedience: Adam wished 'to be free,' he refused to submit. In reality it is just the opposite that happened: having tasted of the fruits of the tree of knowledge, man lost the freedom he possessed on

leaving the hands of the Creator and became the slave of
'the eternal truths'.[3]

Thus we have a spectrum of knowledge: from absolute prohibition on the one hand to the absolute constraints of reason on the
other. This spectrum contains the 'Thou shalt not' at the darkest
end to the lucid brilliance of $2 + 2 = 4$ at the other. The one forbids; the other compels.

Is there a middle ground, a knowledge involving freely-given
consent to relation, a voluntary constraint?

The Covenant

The Covenant is the heart of biblical epistemology. It is the fourth
act of the drama after Creation, Temptation, and Fall have occurred. But the first three acts of the drama take place in 'metaphysical' time, a time in which the 'having occurred' and the
'occurring' are simultaneous. The fourth act of the drama is occurring in genealogical time; for us, it is forever how the action
'will occur.' Covenant is the promise of futurity. Eugene Rosenstock-Huessy compresses the covenantal idea into the whole notion of revelation:

> Revelation is knowledge of God's will, after his 'No' to
> our will has become known. Only then is God pure future,
> pure act — only when all his former creations stand
> exposed as non-gods, as mere artifacts.[4]

Covenant, which means 'promise' or 'agreement,' is a form-
alization of the *is*. That is to say, the character of the 'is,' the word
which indicates mutuality and common agreement, is *revealed*.
It is being in time. The covenant is the harnessing of thinking to
this being in time, to this mutuality. Even to 'think-about-think-
ing' otherwise than by means of this harness in time, is, literally,
a 'waste of time.'[5] Covenant is the consent to being harnessed
in time, the consent to historical being, the consent to being

historical. Man freely acknowledges the constraint which his being in time puts upon him. Man consents to this constraint voluntarily — not because 2 + 2 compels his consent, nor because God forbids him not to consent. Covenant is the middle ground between the compulsion of rational truth and the prohibition of God's absolute will.

Mutuality defines the human being's relationship to nature and to God. In Genesis the idea of Covenant first dawns in Genesis in connection with the idea of stewardship. In Genesis 1:28 God blesses his new creation, man, and says 'Be fruitful, and multiply ... and have dominion over the fish of the sea ... and every living thing.' In Genesis 2:15 God places man in the Garden of Eden, 'to dress it and keep it.' In Genesis 9:9f the covenantal idea becomes even more urgent, when after the Flood that destroyed the earth, God tells Noah that 'I establish my covenant with you, and with your seed after you, and with every living creature that is with you ...'

The figure of Noah is a turning point. With Noah we begin to make a first turn from nature into history — from the natural to the historical covenant. Noah is a sort of saviour-figure of nature. Mankind has not been doing too well since the Fall, and there is that wonderful phrase, which rolls off the tongue with biblical sonorousness: 'And God saw that the wickedness of man was great upon the earth, and that every imagination of the thoughts of his heart was only evil continually.' (Gen.6:5) God unleashes his Flood to cancel what appears to be a wrong start, but tells Noah to build the ark and to bring in representatives, two by two, of the animal kingdom.

The saving of the creatures is a kind of recollection of nature or of man's 'natural self.' Recollection is a creative gesture which precedes the appearance of any new historical impulse. We can find many examples of creative recollection in history. The Renaissance humanists 'recollected' themselves, not so much in nature as such, but in a nature transmitted by classical Greek and Roman culture. The Puritan founders of the Massachusetts Bay colony in America believed that they were establishing a New Jerusalem. The Rev Martin Luther King, Jr. forged a bond with Moses and called the new dispensation of race relations in Amer-

ica the 'promised land.' The Romantic poet Wordsworth recollected himself as a 'natural being' when he said:

> There was a time, when every meadow, grove, and stream
> When earth, and every common sight to me did seem
> Apparelled in celestial light ...

He was calling forth in poetry something from the deepest layers
of memory, from the world of 'there was a time.'

It is interesting to consider what happened to this Romantic
recollection in the modern era. What is the essence of modernity?
Modernity is the concept of 'natural being' without the creative
recollection. When Freud remarked, in *Civilization and Its Dis-
contents,* that 'Civilization is built upon the renunciation of instinct,' and 'Every individual is virtually an enemy of
civilization,' these remarks looked back to Wordsworth. But it
was to a Wordsworth without the poetry. The 'natural being' of
romanticism had been revived, but without recollection. Natural-
ness, instinctivity, the primitive, had become a thing, a something,
a 'human nature.' Primitiveness in itself becomes an important
theme in modernity — the primitive in intellectualized, rather
than recollected, form.

There is a curious incident in the life of Noah, which points to
the problem that arises when this 'natural being' is confronted
without reticence or recollection. After the Flood, Noah becomes
a vineyardman, and in the course of drinking wine, he falls asleep
in his tent, naked. His son Ham 'sees the nakedness of his father.'
(Gen.9:22) For reasons we may find difficult to understand, the
sight of the raw generational fact is a kind of horror. It is a little
bit similar to the Medusa of Greek mythology. Although he is
not turned to stone, Ham is 'cursed.' The covenantal idea and the
generational fact have yet to be united, far into the future, with
Abraham.

In the many generations intervening between Noah and Abraham, the one significant event, the Tower of Babel incident, is
mentioned. The whole earth at the time was of one language, and
mankind aspired to construct a tower to heaven. This ambitious
project was watched by God with great consternation: 'And the

Lord said, Behold, the people is one, and they have all one language; and this they begin to do: and now nothing will be re-
strained from them, which they have imagined to do.' (Gen.11:6)

This passage describes our world, united in the universal language of mathematics and science. There are still a multiplicity of
languages upon the earth. But in fact the language of scientific
and technological accomplishment unites almost all the peoples
of the earth, if not in actuality then in aspiration. In the biblical
story, God 'confounds the language' of mankind, so that there
should not be too great a concentration of power. God causes a
natural constraint to be placed amid the peoples of the earth.

Such 'natural constraints' are hard to find today. Ethnic strife
divides and confounds modern nations. Such strife may always
have existed, but its intensity and bitterness may be something of
a symptomatic reaction against the abstract universal language of
modernity, rationality, and science. In any case modern man looks
in vain for God or nature to constrain him. Modern man must
teach himself the language of voluntary constraint, the language
of covenant.

Approaching Abraham

Abraham persists through the tolling of forty centuries to stare at
us, question us, challenge us, counsel us, lead the way, beckon,
plead, intercede, fight, stand, remain: Abraham is there at the
crossroads, he is sitting at the door of his tent, he is offering us,
the strangers, his hospitality, his substance.

Abraham, first known as Abram, is waiting; acting, being
guided in action; leaving Ur; going to Canaan; leaving Canaan,
going to Egypt; waiting, waiting. Abraham is childless. He leaves
his kindred behind in the glorious city, the first city, the Ur-city;
he divides himself from Lot, his kinsman; he cleaves unto Sarai,
his wife, his sister (by his father, not his mother) who is infertile.

We don't know much about Sarai, who later becomes Sarah. As
a female character, she is less defined than those who come after:
Rebekah, Rachel, Leah, Tamar, Ruth ... The women of the Old

Testament have immense dignity and hidden power. Sarai laughs when the three strangers come and prophesy that she will bear a son to Abraham. (Gen.18:12) But the name of the son who is born, Isaac, means 'laughter.' There is thus a tiny hint of humour injected into this whole enterprise between God and man, or rather God, man, and woman. The dignified and justifiable patriarchalism of the Bible needs this touch of humour, which comes even more to the fore in the love-story of Jacob and the fun-loving, rascally Rachel.

The Covenant is revealed to Abraham in stages, but one important moment of this revelation occurs when Abraham is in his ninety-ninth year. At that time God came to him and revealed himself as God the 'Almighty' — more exactly, the God with breasts, *El Shaddai.* The Hebrew word, *shad,* means breast, like a woman's breast that soothes and suckles. And God as El Shaddai says to Abraham: 'I will make my covenant between thee and me, and will multiply thee exceedingly' (Gen.17:2). At that time the rite of circumcision was instituted.

Many of the themes we have discussed previously converge in this moment of the biblical story. There is the generational theme of 30 (or 33) — 99 being a multiple of thirty-three. It is as if Abraham has to live for almost a whole century, passing through three generations, before he and Sarah become able to conceive together. Conceiving is not the natural and automatic thing we often take it to be — and in our materialized age, the job is up to the eggs, the sperm, and their general effectiveness in uniting to pass on our genes.[6] True, both human beings and fruit flies 'pass on their genes.' But human beings pass on something else as well. Human beings must have something to pass on, that is, not just genes, but rather the crystallized understanding deriving from the encounter of their interiority with the world.

Reproduction, for human beings, involves telling the story of one's life. In the Bible this connection between reproduction and story-telling is so intimate, so intricate, that to us, it almost appears a form of madness! Abraham, Isaac, and Jacob are as much the founders of a nation as they are founts of story-telling. 'Very deep is the well of the past,' begins Thomas Mann in *Joseph and His Brothers,* 'Should we not call it bottomless?' The story of Joseph begins with recapitulating the stories of Jacob, Abraham, Noah, Adam, God. 'This is the book of the generations of Adam' (Gen.5:1) and 'These are the generations of the heavens and of the earth' (Gen.2:4).[7] Being in the generations is having a story to tell.

God as the 'nourisher,' the God with Breasts, is a challenge to those who dismiss the Bible as merely a patriarchal document. The patriarchalism of the Bible accompanies its matriarchalism. The one concept is void without the other. The patriarchs and matriarchs interact with each other and with God in different ways, with sometimes opposing (or complementary) but 'equal' powers. Those who read the Bible as a patriarchal document seem to want to have the matriarchs be just like the patriarchs, the women just like the men — for there to be no difference or distinction between them.

It is no accident that the statement of the Covenant comes about when God appears to Abraham in this powerfully female form. God Himself seems to be saying something as Herself. What is the message here?

The Covenant is that form of knowledge in which distinction and relation co-exist. That which 'holds' them in co-existence is time — historical time. This historical time is not only a 'was'; it is also the 'will be.' The critical juncture between 'was' and 'will be' is participation. God's appearance to Abraham as the God of Breasts may be compared with the birth of Athena, Greek goddess of wisdom, who sprang fully formed from the head of Zeus. But the Hebraic image of the feminine is also very unlike the Greek. The Greek goddess was an image of thought, fully-formed. Athena had no childhood. *El Shaddai,* on the other hand, emphasizes the period of suckling and dependency which precedes the thinking life of any human being — male or female. Now this image of childhood dependency appears not just in God the father, but in God as mother. This image is extremely significant for female participation in the covenant.

Childhood is the basis for the development of human intelligence. Even the feminists, who have been only too ready to condemn the Bible and Western history for its patriarchal bias, have been conspicuously silent on the problem raised by the biological fact that girls mature earlier than boys. We do not, even today, tend to associate femininity with childhood. 'Boys will be boys.' But girls will be — what? Girls will grow up too soon — a tendency already accelerated by the over-sexualized imagery of popular culture.[8] For feminists to condemn biblical morality as demeaning to women is short-sighted. Biblical morality — chastity and restraint in sexual matters — is, for a woman (even more than for a man) essential to the preservation, development, and refinement of the thinking capacity. Biblical morality is not the sign of women's exclusion but of their participation.

The Abrahamic Covenant

Covenant, which means 'promise' or 'agreement,' grants ontological status, metaphysical standing, realness, reality, genuine being, individuality, and so on, to each party in the compact. The covenant says that the idea of mutuality is not inconsistent with the idea of individuality. In fact the two ideas are themselves covenanted together.

Part of the Abrahamic covenant can be worked out syllogistically. It goes something like this:

   a. Covenant is a free relationship.

   b. To be in covenant relation implies the existence of things or beings with which, or to which, one is in relation. In the same way, covenant relation also implies being in oneself, a being that is oneself, which is in relation to these other things or beings.

   c. Covenant relation, therefore, says that through mutuality not only the world with its beings and things is real, but also the individual is real.

   d. Covenant relation, therefore, grants ontological status to mutuality andindividuality.

Mutuality is not the same thing as 'totality,' or 'merging together' or 'blending' or 'transcendence' or 'higher resolution.' It is hard to keep a firm grip on the idea of mutuality, just as it is hard to grasp the idea of individuality. Neither in thinking nor in life can the concepts be had without each other. Yet the tendency in thinking is to lose the grasp of them together, and for both of them to go wriggling and swimming away into some larger ocean of transcendence. Or, on the other hand, thinking may eliminate the problem altogether because it is just too difficult, and make the claim that individuality is not a problem because it doesn't enter into the equation of the determined world, the world of generality, species, and prediction.

The religious thought of the East seems to be attracted to the first option; the scientific thought of the West gravitates towards the second. Along the same lines, spirituality grants dignity to human life, but sometimes at the price of taking man outside of history. A biological or deterministic view, on the other hand, leaves man on earth and in history, but without the dignity of the divine connection.

The Abrahamic Covenant keeps man on earth and in history but retains the dignity of connection. It does this by focusing our minds on the problem of individuality and mutuality to an inescapable and almost unbearable degree of intensity. Especially is this true in the part of Abraham's story that deals with Isaac.

After years of infertility and waiting, a son is born to Abraham and Sarah. This prelude makes all the more incomprehensible the passage in Genesis where it says that God 'tempts' Abraham: 'Take now thy son, thine only son, Isaac, whom thou lovest, and get thee into the land of Moriah, and offer him there for a burnt-offering upon one of the mountains I will tell thee of.' (Gen.22:2)

The Sacrifice *(Akedah)* or 'Binding' of Isaac is one of those stories in mankind's cultural history which exists on the borders of understanding. Indeed, it is almost impossible to understand — and not only for the rational mind, but for any kind of mind. Is it a myth? Is God jealous of Abraham's love for Isaac? Is it God revealing himself as a bloodthirsty tyrant rather than as a loving partner in covenant relation? Is it a 'perpetual reenacted radical surprise' (Emil Fackenheim) or the 'teleological suspension of the ethical' (Kierkegaard)?

No wonder that Silvano Arieti, a distinguished psychiatrist, commented that 'On becoming acquainted with the story for the first time, one is struck with astonishment and trepidation ... the resonance and mystery of [this] episode put it in a class by itself.'[9]

He quotes Elie Wiesel: '... Here is a story that contains Jewish destiny in its totality, just as the flame is contained in the single spark by which it comes to life. Every major theme, every passion and obsession that make Judaism the adventure that it is, can be traced back to it.'

Kierkegaard's essay on the Abraham-Isaac story, *Fear and Trembling,* puts emotional intensity — the 'distress and anxiety in the paradox of faith' — in the centre. Kierkegaard called Abraham the Knight of Faith, a man essentially obedient to God.[10] For the sake of this *telos,* that is, purpose, Abraham was led to suspend the moral law which says that a father should love his son. This moral law is what Kierkegaard means by *the ethical.* Abraham's obedience to God was, therefore, the 'teleological suspension of the ethical.' In Kierkegaard's words, 'The Knight of Faith is completely abandoned to himself, and it is in this that the horror of his situation consists.' Lev Shestov, in commenting on this, says that 'Abraham ... is above all, for Kierkegaard, a man driven out of the universal and therefore deprived of the protection of universal and necessary truths.'[11]

We are in a realm of absolutes, of ultimates. In this story, Abraham represents the single individual who '... stands in an absolute relation to the absolute.'

The story puts a strain upon our minds. We cannot run away from it; we must walk toward it, although we cannot walk toward it willingly. Everything about this confrontation goes against our love — which is, first of all, the desire that we should have a future, that the future should be realized in us. The biblical covenant of mutuality is always colliding with individuality, with the raw, stubborn fact of individual being. If I am myself as I am, what 'will be' can be vouchsafed to me? And if I 'will be,' what am I in my I am?

God made a covenant with Abraham to provide him with descendants. Yet when God demands Abraham to sacrifice this son of the covenant, an unbearable contradiction arises. To kill Isaac is to kill off the promise of legitimate descendants. Not to kill Isaac would mean to forsake God's command, and therefore, the relationship with God on which the covenant is based. But with either choice, the covenant is broken: either in the sense of

physical descendants (genealogy) or in the sense of the God-rela-
tion (metaphysics).

Is it a test of mutual exclusion? — If you love Isaac, you do not
love God. If you love God, you do not love Isaac. Simone Weil
once said: 'Contradiction is the instrument of transcendence.' The
Abraham-Isaac story is an unbearable contradiction. But the contradiction is resolved not in the sense of transcendence but in the
sense of history. How the rescue of history comes about when
facts, logic, and even divine commandment seem to be stacked
against it will be the focus of our next inquiry.

The Ransom

The Viennese psychiatrist Erich Wellisch wrote a book, *Isaac and
Oedipus* (1956) comparing the Isaac-tale in the Old Testament to
the Greek myth of Oedipus. Silvano Arieti discusses Wellisch's
insights in his *Abraham and the Contemporary Mind*. As might
be expected, Wellisch's arguments detail psychological motifs:
the main motive for infanticide by fathers is the unwillingness of
fathers 'to give up their absolute superiority for the benefit of
growing children.' Wellisch argued that 'until Abraham the
father's authority was based on fear. Since Abraham it has been
based on love.'[12]

I think that Wellisch's comparison of Isaac and Oedipus is
deeply insightful, although for reasons epistemological and historical rather than psychological. The stories are in many ways
polar opposites of each other. In the Greek story, there is no history, properly speaking; there is only fate. Oedipus tries to placate
the gods; he leaves the city of his youth, Corinth, in order not to
fulfill the oracle, which foretold at his birth that he would kill his
father and marry his mother. He does everything humanly possible to avert his fate, but, in the end, it still comes crashing down
upon him with inexorable force.

In the biblical story, on the other hand, Abraham does everything he can possibly do to honour his human part of God's
covenant. Kierkegaard emphasized in particular this quality of

Abrahamic 'obedience.' Abraham is a partner with God, in conversation with God, obedient to God. And yet God's command to take Isaac to a mountain and offer him as a burnt-offering comes crashing down upon Abraham like a bolt from the blue, a torpedo from an unfathomable will. But in the end the jaws of contradiction are pried open. God tells Abraham to offer a ram in place of Isaac. Abraham's obedience to God has been tested, and Abraham has passed the test. Isaac is saved; the line of generations will go on. History continues.

The demand of the hour, the *what-is* in time, and the decision, on Abraham's part, to deal with it: this is what is meant by 'obedience to God.' For the Bible speaks a veiled language when it says, as the story opens, that the Lord 'tempted' Abraham. For man's temptation is to refuse his circumstances for the sake of his 'values.' Two values confronted Abraham: the love of God and the love of his son. By bringing these values into heightened conflict, the biblical story shows that the love of truth — that is, the determination, on the part of man, to deal with his circumstances, whatever they are at the moment — can lead, not to the abandonment of either values or circumstances, but their resolution and accommodation.

Before asking how fate is averted and history happens, let us review what we have learned so far. Our overall question is how thought, the essential expression of our interiority, meets actuality, and how this meeting of thought and actuality leads to mankind and historical life. In approaching this question, we have broken our inquiry down into various chunks in order to manage it better. We have discussed thinking as the essential mode of paying attention in the introduction and Chapter One; thought and personal being in Chapter Two; thought and the temptation story in Chapter Three; thought and time-process in Chapter Four; thought and incarnated life in Chapter Five; and thought as concept and percept embodied in the story of Cain and Abel in Chapter Six.

Now let us return to the temptation story. Let us stand, once again, before the tree of knowledge of good and evil. For after all, we began this book with the symbolism of the serpent, which, it was suggested, has something to do with human cognitive and imaginative capacity. It may seem, that in all this discussion about thinking, that we have left the serpent behind. It is not so. The serpent is twining its way, accompanying us through this book. We still have a gift to receive from the serpent — a gift from which we must do our best to remove, or at least antidote, the poison. We need to return to the Garden of Eden because what is happening there is still happening. The Garden of Eden is a metaphysical postulate. The Garden of Eden is the only thing in the Bible which is immune from time. When we realize this, it only allows us to experience real time more poignantly, to realize that despite all of the fulfilment and richness and fullness and sadness in real time, there is a gulf between 'then' and 'now.' But the 'then' of the Garden of Eden is not in some past, not even in some past of myth. That 'then' is, in a manner of speaking, our 'now,' just as our 'now' is always slipping behind us.[13]

The Garden of Eden brings to the forefront the particular problem of language and symbolism in human life. Language and symbolism are both enormous topics of modern philosophical concern. It seems that hardly had we human beings begun to 'be preoccupied with the phenomena themselves' — to speak Barfield's language (compare Chapter One) — than we began to be concerned with the *words* we were using in which to express these preoccupations.

Modern philosophers ask questions such as the following: Have we any notion of what things are like before we make contact with them? Are the divisions made by our vocabulary really alien to the natures of those things? Is there any way of getting between language and the world to find out if there is a general fit between them or a general misfit?

These questions were asked by a reviewer in the May 19, 1986, issue of the magazine, *The New Republic,* in an article about Ludwig Wittgenstein, a philosopher preoccupied with the question of meaning. The questions make us a little dizzy; they remind us of a serpent clutching its own tail in its mouth. Wittgenstein proved himself to be a step ahead of his commentators when he made the marvellous statement that: 'A philosopher is a man who has to cure many intellectual diseases in himself before he can arrive at notions of common sense.'[14]

It is easy to get lost in the fog of symbol, sign, word, meaning, referent, connotation, denotation, etc. A refined discussion of these matters is not only beyond my power; it is also beyond the purposes of this book. Our purpose is to understand what symbolism may mean generally in terms of biblical epistemology and specifically in terms of the covenant.

The word 'symbol' is derived from the Greek, *sym* or *(syn)*, 'with' + *ballein,* 'to throw.' A symbol is that which unites or 'throws together.'

Susanne K. Langer, a philosopher of language, believed that one of the most important discoveries of the twentieth century was that of the universal symbolizing faculty of the human mind. In commenting upon A.D. Ritchie's remark that 'The essential act of thought is its symbolization,' Langer replied: 'As a matter of fact, it is not the essential act of thought that is symbolization, but an act *essential to thought* and prior to it.'[15]

I have a brother named John. When I say 'John' it denotes my brother, and it is through this denotation that I can talk about John even when this John is not present. 'John' offers itself as a substitute for John, the real person, my brother, who lives far away in Argentina. It is by means of 'John' for John that I can recall this person to myself, talk about him in the presence of others.

This is what a symbol does: it gives or offers one thing in place of another. I can point to John, if he is standing there; but I cannot point to 'John' in the same way. 'John' allows a whole new world to come into being with respect to thoughts about John — what he was like as a child, how we were together as children, what he is like now, my memories of him and hopes for him. When in the presence of family and friends, 'John' allows mutual corroboration of our perceptions and thoughts relating to John.

Symbolic facility allows the world of verification, mutuality and corroboration to come into being. In this way we keep grounded in the world and in touch with other people. Language permits us to substitute a symbol for something real.

But this substitution of symbol for something real is, in terms of the biblical story of the temptation, problematic. Modern language philosophers, in exploring the wonderful things that symbols can do, and in explaining how necessary symbols are for our thinking life, have tended to overlook this sober reminder from Genesis. Things are not always as wonderful as they seem. Indeed, in many ways the Abraham- Isaac story throws us into a quagmire of symbolism. What is the meaning of the terms freedom, obedience, identity, individuality, mutuality, even covenant? Are we living a life or are we pursuing a meaning — however close to the real heartbeat of life that meaning may be? In the Abraham story intellectual and vital reason come into titanic struggle — all the more titanic for being so hard to pin down, so inward, so subtle. For it is God himself who pins himself down for us, a God who shrinks himself into an atomic dot — a God who even mocks the serpent by calling his demand upon Abraham a 'temptation.'

This is the God who says symbolism is not enough. This God demands that we substitute something real for the symbol.

* * * *

It is the act of ransom — 'the action of procuring release of a prisoner or captive by paying a price; or of obtaining one's own freedom in this way' — that gives man the assurance that his thinking is real, that it has a purpose, that it can bear fruit, that history may continue.

The Ram appears in the thicket — the dialectical muddle, the briar-patch of symbolical concepts. Is this some kind of *deus ex machina,* that the ram should appear just at the right moment to save the life of Isaac, spare Abraham from having to commit murder upon what he loves, and preserve the Covenant for one hundred and twenty future generations? Is this ransoming of Isaac a stage-trick that closes the dramatic life of Abraham, a puff of smoke and magic to confound our epistemological striving?

Let us return, for a moment, to the forked tongue of the serpent. One of the most useful ideas to be developed out of the spiritual science or anthroposophy of Rudolf Steiner is clarification regarding the nature of the Tempter — the Devil.

Diabolos, the name of the tempter, derives from the Greek *dia,* 'two' + *ballein,* 'to throw.' *Diabolism* is a splitting-into-two, whereas *symbolism* is a making-into-one. The covenant is threatened by *Diabolos* from two sides. Rudolf Steiner assigns the names Lucifer and Ahriman to this *Diaballein* — the 'hot' and the 'cold' forms of it respectively. Although Diabolos is not mentioned by name in this biblical story of Abraham and Isaac, I will use the names (of Lucifer and the more traditionally biblical Satan) for purposes of discussion.

God, through the command to Abraham to sacrifice Isaac, calls the devil(s) out into the open air to confuse them. The ransom, the giving of the ram in place of Isaac, may be understood as that which becomes possible when the devils are confused, when they must contend against each other and not with man. An opening is created whereby the toil of yesterday may become the fruit of today, and the fruit of today may become the seed for tomorrow. The *metaphysical* and the *genealogical,* stretched to the maximum point of tension, may become the *historical.*

For at all times Satan wants to claim man's toil and Lucifer wants to claim man's fruit. What is the danger in terms of the covenant? Lucifer wants the covenant to be fruitful: but he wants it to be *me* or *mine.* Satan does not care whose covenant it is; but he does not want it to be *fruitful.*

Any act of continuity, of fruitfulness following upon original act, must address these double perils, these temptations arising from two sides. The action of these beings expresses our historical reality, of what we are up against in our historical life.

But in the biblical story, not even between the fire and the knife, is the Tempter's double name revealed. The Tempter either lives in Paradise or Hell. But history continually confounds and eludes him.

Symbol as Ransom

Biblical epistemology increases in complexity but not abstraction. It thus moves in a direction contrary to rational philosophy, which begins with abstraction and moves toward simplification, e.g., reductionism.

It is difficult to add complexity and depth to one's thinking while maintaining the purity of intention never to forsake the ground lands of the concrete. It can be done, but only with a commitment to developing moral imagination and historical consciousness while striving, above all else, for a fierce clarity.

In the Abraham-Isaac story the Ram is given in place of Isaac. Something real is substituted for the symbol. In Christian theology this Old Testament story is often held to be a prefiguring of the story of Jesus Christ. The significance of Jesus for biblical epistemology is that the ransoming process is carried to a further stage. Symbolism itself becomes the ransom of the real. The absolute limit of symbolism was reached when Christian doctrine said that Jesus is the ransom of the world, not only our human, historical world, but the whole world, the cosmic world.

This is an extraordinary claim to make, so extraordinary that only Christians, presumably, believe it. Christians had to become believers if they were to be Christians — a paradox which continues to be as hard to swallow now as it has been through history. This claim is why Christianity has a theology, and Judaism, properly speaking, does not. The story of Christian theology is the unending struggle between Christianity and belief.

Judaism never needed to wrestle with the problem of belief. Judaism meant belonging to the Abrahamic covenant. The problem of belonging versus belief arose with Christianity, and the relations between Christianity and Judaism eventually soured because the struggle between the theology of Christianity and the covenant of Judaism was so great and so seemingly insoluble.

Biblical epistemology acknowledges the unique epistemological significance of Jesus but says that this unique significance also belongs to the covenant. Thus biblical epistemology takes the question to its historical limit and in so doing re-opens it to the infinite.

In attempting to show why this extraordinary theological claim about Jesus was made by Christians, we can only attempt to clarify the epistemological situation that led up to it. Biblical epistemology cannot say whether or not to believe it. But in examining it, biblical epistemology suggests that this belief, like any other, is a form of knowledge which does not expose itself to the outdoors, to the historical, to the infinite. Belief is knowledge for shut-ins. Thus the question that epistemologists are always asking, 'How can knowledge be distinguished from belief?' — is a little off the mark. Knowledge cannot be defined apart from a time-process. *Knowledge is how we digest belief,* and everything is a belief until we have put it through the digestive process, that is, until we have undergone the process of living it.

That is why the Tempter tries so hard to prevent us from living our history. The Tempter always wants to seduce us into living a form of thought that has already been thought, or a form of thought undetermined as yet otherwise than by me. The Tempter thus always slides back and forth between either freezing our history or inflating our own wishes, desires, self-importance. Thus the Tempter's 'Ye shall be as gods!' sounds as mockery in our ears. Yes, as Gods — but on a frozen sea of time. The Tempter would poison that in us which seeks to become historically creative.

The Jews subjected themselves to the time-process, the covenant. The Christians subjected themselves to belief (or revolted against this subjection to belief). Belief in Christianity, by seeming to take precedence over the Covenant, accentuated what was already a tendency in the rationalism that Christian thought inherited from the Greeks — that is, an abstraction from time. Both from Greek philosophy and Christian belief our Western world received a double dose of abstract rationalism.

The result? Rationalistic dissection and religious sect-making, the continuous fissioning of history, cutting and division and now, in the late twentieth century, an aggressive sexuality that has been made to carry the weight of politics, ideology and identity.[16]

The task of biblical epistemology is to gather these divided fragments back into a meaning — to pronounce something other than scatteration upon human destiny.

* * * *

Let us return to the Judean-Galilean landscape, so rich in symbolical meanings, to the figure of Jesus striding across it, most often in conversation with one or two others. Let us imaginatively transport this figure to the terrain of modern philosophy, perhaps not as rich in geological meaning as Palestine, but rich nonetheless in the human striving to derive certainty from the knowledge we have from merely living a life in the world.

Realism and idealism are the two poles of philosophy. Realism says that when thinking encounters the actuality of the world, the things that it meets up with are actually there. What you see is what you get. Descartes came along and said that it is indubitably true that we are thinking, but what do we really know by means of it? The central thing is the thinking. This is the point of view of idealism.

This thought was digested in various ways in the philosophical tradition. Locke (born 1632) came along and said that we don't know anything except what has been placed before in our senses. The Scotsman Hume (born 1711) objected, and said the only thing we can know about our knowing is that it takes place in a mental state. Custom and the association of ideas lead us to deduce truths, such as the idea of substance or causality.

Hume's objections to Locke roused Immanuel Kant (born 1724) from his 'dogmatic slumber,' as this philosopher said of himself. The dogma in question was the contention of realism, or rather, of empiricism — that is, that the things in our minds do corroborate with the things in the world and that reality is to be known through the 'given.'[17] It is interesting that Kant thought of empiricism or realism as a 'dogma,' so at odds with current connotations of the word. Nevertheless, he set out to rescue the pure reason from this collision with actuality, and the way he went about it was to put the burden of proof upon the reason rather than on the data of the world.

Kant distinguished two main statements of knowledge, the analytic statement and the synthetic statement. The analytic statement contains the predicate in the subject: e.g., a bachelor is an unmarried male. As long as you know the meaning of 'bachelor,' you will know for all time that it is an 'unmarried male.'

A synthetic statement, on the other hand, puts a subject and predicate together without an obvious means of connecting them, e.g., 'Water boils at 212°F at sea level.' In order to connect the subject and predicate in this statement, you have to have sense-data. But what is the guarantee that this statement will be true for all time? Kant's question was, then, How are synthetic *a priori* statements possible? — *a priori* meaning that which is necessary and true for all time.[18]

Kant's answer was to say that we can't know what the thing in itself really is, but only as the phenomenon is made by the team-work with our own minds. Our minds (the noumenal or mental world) organize the data of the phenomenal or real world through the 'categories,' the important ones being time, space, and causality. Although there really is a world out there, the organizing power of the human mind calls the shots.

Modern language philosophies took the Kantian organizing power of the categories into a further stage. As the real world seemed to grow more and more distant, a 'something there' laboriously translated only by means of our own minds, the question of language and symbolism became more and more important. If we were not really connecting with the world, how were we connecting with language? How was communication itself possible? What was the nature of the symbolical world of language in which we found ourselves? Language, that is, the 'symbolical forms' became a mental category: '... it is not reality which is known but the symbolic forms through which reality is conceived.'[19]

But if this is so, what about the reality of our identity? As Walker Percy puts it:

> ... the requirement of consciousness that everything *be* something and willy-nilly everything *is* something — *with one tremendous exception!* The one thing in the world which by its very nature is not susceptible to stable symbolic transformation is *myself!* I, who symbolize the world in order to know it, am destined to remain forever unknowable to myself.[20]

In addressing this problem of stable identity, of the 'I,' it is important to remember that biblical epistemology deals with not one, but two, forms of time. In Adamic time we may ask this question about the real and symbolical, and the serpent will hold his own tail in his mouth and go around in circles forever.

Metaphysical time ultimately begets despair. We cannot perceive how we are born into it, much less escape it. There is something of a Garden of Eden experience in this 'I' that is held in suspension; Paradise and Temptation forever surround it.

But because we can never know in advance what circumstances will demand from us, living a life in history can never be theoretical. It is this fact which forces us to the limiting edge of concreteness; it is this fact which thrusts us into Abrahamic time. We *are* born into Abrahamic time; and in Abrahamic time we get to Jesus. And with Jesus we get to Golgotha, the Place of the Skull. At Golgotha Jesus cries the question: 'My God, my God, why have you forsaken me?' Why have you abandoned me to historical suffering? It was the dramatic power of this 'symbolical' event which had become historical which gave to the early Christians the conviction that Christ had conquered the demons.

There was an old legend that said the wood from the Tree of Knowledge was used to build the Cross on Golgotha. It is true in the sense that what was a problem of knowledge in Genesis became resolved by the Cross in the New Testament. The Cross says that how people cognize in history answers the problem first set out in the Garden of Eden. In other words, cognition has become historical, and this historical element is its saving grace; it is the part that can 'deliver us from evil.' The Cross is the ransoming of symbolism by an event in time so particular and contingent that it is a reproach to the philosophic intellect. Indeed, it is difficult to linger on the edge of moral imagination that is the story of the Cross. One's impulse is either to keep climbing up one side — like the edge of a knife — in the toils of Theology, or fall over to the other side into unbelief.

Both of these alternatives fall short of a biblical epistemology, which is the attempt to make a place for both Covenant and Cross. The threads of linkage between the two lead all the way to the Modern Age and to some of its most vexing issues.

Chapter Eight

The Coming Age

Seeing Abysses

The theme of the abyss sounds in the New Testament. At the Baptism Jesus goes down into the Jordan valley, the lowest place on the earth. The Place of the Baptism, where the Jordan River empties into the Dead Sea, is an abyss, 1290 feet below sea level.[1]

The theme of the abyss haunts modern thought. It is the geological-spiritual metaphor for the situation of modern man, the place of 'maximum disinvestment' that Andrew Delbanco talked about in *The Death of Satan.* Nietzsche once declared: 'Is not seeing itself — seeing abysses?' Gertrude Himmelfarb, in a book aptly entitled *On Looking into the Abyss,* discussed the work of Nietzsche, Freud, Dostoevsky, Heidegger, and the modernists whose books were 'profoundly subversive of culture, society, morality, conventional sexuality — and of all that which was once confidently called "civilization".'

There was also Edmund Husserl (1859–1938), the founder of the philosophical school of phenomenology, who paid tribute to the 'abyss' in his book, *The Crisis of European Science,* when he wrote:

> The life-world is the realm of original self-evidences ... If we cease being immersed in our scientific thinking, we become aware that we scientists are, after all, human beings, and as such are among the components of the life-world

which always exists for us pre-given ... The paradoxical
interrelationships of the 'objectively true world' and the
'life world' make enigmatic the manner of being of both ...
In our attempts to gain clarity we shall suddenly become
aware ... *that all our philosophizing up to now has been
without a ground.*

The abyss is the place of *conceptual death,* Would there not be
a *Temptation* — that, because man stands upon *nothing,* as it were
— in that he stands in *history* — would there not be a temptation
to collapse 'All the kingdoms of the world in a moment of time'?
(Luke 4:5) The deconstructive paradox! We are in an abundant
world, the mass media-ization of the historical, but conceiving,
wielding symbolism, without getting to the *is.* 'What was simply
referential text now becomes the text of a text, the figure of a
figure.'[2] 'There is no such thing as intrinsic value,' Stanley Fish
declared, aiming to dispel the notion of a 'within,' a meaning to it
all, a 'ground of Being.'

Philosophical nihilism, deconstructive seduction, technological
allurement: indeed, is there anything missing in the story of the
Temptation for late twentieth-century man? Is it not here in a nut-
shell ... an historical parable?

But somehow, the moment of Temptation passes and Jesus continues on his way.

But — what have we here? Soon afterwards — as recounted in
the Luke Gospel — we find Jesus taking an axe to the tree of
Covenant, at least where the Covenant has to do with the idea of
a chosen people. For what could be more challenging philosophically to the idea of being 'Chosen' — saved, set apart, distinguished — than the Beatitudes in the sixth chapter of Luke?
'Blessed are ye poor ... Blessed are ye that hunger ... Blessed are
ye, when men shall hate you ... Woe unto ye, when all men shall
speak well of you! ... Woe unto you that are full! ... '

What is this but the 'privileging,' as the deconstructionists like
to say, of human lack, limitation, incompleteness, unfulfilment,
not-having ...? What is this renunciation in the New Testament?

Fullness and Renunciation

The renunciation that Jesus made, the 'No!' that he said, was a shock that has not ceased to reverberate over twenty centuries. 'No!' is not *nothing*. It is the serpent who makes this equivalence for us, the serpent who whispers: 'No ... It is nothing ... It does not matter ... *It is only an idea!'* The serpent derives the nothing from the No, and spits the No back at us in the form of a Nothing. In this way he mocks even himself. For he does not stand upright even in his No!, but says it, spits it, and then slides away from us, quickly, before we have had a chance to grasp it.

The 'No!' that Jesus speaks is a sweeping of the decks, a reaming out, a scouring and a fumigation of the atmosphere. This scouring, fumigating and emptying-out is how original act is experienced in the historical world. For it is only too true that there can be no authentic originality in the historical world. Something has always gone before.

The passing of the Old Testament into the New, the birth of Christianity from the parent stock of Judaism, the Cross and the empty tomb: these events divide time itself into two parts, before and after. What transpired in the era of the *pax romana,* roughly a 100-year period lasting from about 70 BC to AD 30, represents such a heating-up and coagulation of forces in history that it may be compared with the forces in the universe that lead to stellar explosions. To a large degree even today, almost everything in our horizon is the result of compromises, conflicts, and complexes established in the three main civilizations of Greek, Roman and Hebrew, and the numerous satellite peoples around them.

Those compromises, conflicts, and complexes eventually settled down into the solar system of the Roman Empire. The barbarian hordes in the North — people who called themselves 'gods' (i.e. Goths) — flung themselves upon the body of this solar system in the fifth century. The sack of Rome in AD 410 is one of those prizes in every cereal box of history, the one we get every year, one of those dates we have no trouble remembering.

The Goths found plenty to digest in Rome. In fact 'gothic' has become a synonym for a type of exaggerated weirdness, weight, heaviness, massiveness, especially in connection with the divine, the occult, and the mysterious. Gothicism is in fact a kind of spiritual digestion, which, in the case of Rome and the West, lasted for about a thousand years. An indication that something mysterious is going on is that, presumably, around AD 500 everybody was speaking Latin, more or less; whereas by AD 1000 they are all speaking French, Italian, Spanish, etc. It is a period of deep, digestive sleep, in which whole new languages are rumbling within.

Well, the Goths are busy digesting, as I have said, and it took about a thousand years to digest Rome, and with it, Judeo-Christianity and Greek philosophy. In 1637 something happened which signified that a halt had been called in this digestive process, that a dramatic turn was being made. Descartes' *Discourse on the Method* was published. Descartes wrote that: '... wished to give myself to the search after Truth. I thought that it was necessary ... to reject as absolutely false everything as to which I could imagine the least ground of doubt, in order to see if afterwards there remained anything in my belief that was entirely certain.' To find truth he subjected everything to doubt, for:

> ... whilst I thus wished to think all things false, it was
> absolutely essential that the 'I' who thought this should be
> somewhat, and remarking that this truth, *'I think, therefore
> I am,'* was so certain and so assured that all the most
> extravagant suppositions brought forward by the skeptics
> were incapable of shaking it, I came to the conclusion that
> I could receive it without scruple as the first principle of
> the Philosophy for which I was seeking.

In other words: everything can be doubted, but the one thing I cannot doubt is that I am doubting. It was a clean sweep, a cleaning of the decks, an emptying-out of everything except the action of emptying-out itself.

Here is something oddly familiar. To find its prototype, we have to go back sixteen centuries, back to the renunciatory 'No!'

of Jesus. This is the concept of *kenosis,* which appears in the theology of St. Paul. It refers to Christ's 'emptying-out' of the divine being in becoming Jesus. 'He did not count equality with God as a thing to be grasped, but emptied himself, taking the form of a servant, being born in the likeness of men.' (Phil.2:6f), Equality with God? Emptying out? Likeness of men? The words and concepts are very strange. These are the first, tender shoots of an idea that did not wholly make it successfully in the world of theology, or rather, an idea that theology has never really been able to know what to do with. That is to say, the part about the 'form of a servant' becomes a theme in the life of Jesus, but the rest of the idea hovers, not fully explicit. Part of this lack of explicitness may have to do with the fact that the theology of Christendom has tended to move away from a full-bodied concept of the spiritual world — a world comprised of hierarchical beings — which, in St. Paul's day, was still a vital notion. This 'emptying-out' or kenosis, then, had to do with Jesus's intention to leave behind a spiritual form of being and take on the historical form of being.

But there might also be more to it than the fact that sixteen centuries after Paul there was no longer any real notion about the hierarchies or about a kenotic self-emptying of them. We have to wait for Descartes for a clarification on this idea of kenosis. And in Descartes the idea is born as a concept of reason, a tool of rationality. Its hierarchical swaddling clothes have been left behind.

For us, the way is open. We can stake a claim on this idea of kenosis, which for us can become a way to address the problem of knowledge.

The kenosis accepts that man has eaten from the tree of knowledge. The point is not whether this food suffices, or seems to suffice for a time, or whether man might eat from the tree of knowledge again, satiating but not nourishing himself. All that is granted. Eating from the tree of knowledge is something we human beings do, because we are historical beings and because our knowledge is incomplete.

It is this incompleteness which to the kenosis, is the significant fact. It is not that *not* eating from the tree of knowledge will make our knowledge complete. *Having a complete knowledge is not even desirable.* Having no knowledge is not possible; having some knowledge is both necessary and desirable in human life. But the distance between the 'none' and the 'some' is infinite. A limit, therefore, applies: for where there is an infinite there is a limit. For 'infinity' transposes the problem from one sphere to another. The 'lack' in human beings which Jesus praises, the emptiness, the clean void: this has to do with the ground between the infinite and the limit. The limit, being reached, indicates that the infinite has become historical. For it is not only the practical kenosis — that having a complete knowledge would not be desirable. *Having a complete knowledge would be the end of history.*

The problem of knowledge is therefore not a problem that can be traversed in quantitative terms. It is not answerable in terms of 'none' and 'some.' It is not answerable in terms of *eating*. For who is to say what is 'some,' what is enough, what suffices, how much is what I need? This is no condemnation of gaining knowledge. What Jesus condemns is gaining knowledge at the price of the infinite — which is, at the price of the historical.

An objector might ask: what has the infinite ever done for me, that I would seek to save a place for the infinite in my knowledge? He might even add that what Jesus says at the Sermon on the Mount appears to be very simple, but this discussion about it is only making the simple complicated. Jesus seems to be saying that it is good to be hungry, not too sure of ourselves, to desire to learn — as the Presbyterian pastor John Lukens explicated the word 'meek' in the phrase 'Blessed are the meek' to mean *educable*. This is very good. It makes sense.

True: all of the above. But I believe that the blessings and condemnations in the Beatitudes (called the Sermon on the Mount in the Matthew Gospel) are also a spiritualized mathematics having to do with historical perspective. In contrast to the Greek spatial geometry of proportion and mean, the Hebrew *logos* of measure pondered temporal limit and infinite.

The discovery of spatial perspective occurred about the time that the 'digestion'of the ancient world was completed, around the 1300s. The discovery blossomed into Renaissance art. What is the art that will spring from the realization of the temporal perspective? We sense that digesting this temporal perspective is an urgent matter, yet for the most part so far it remains an impulse channelled into the drive for material abundance. But digesting this 'daily bread' of temporality and historicity has become necessary and urgent to our life now.

For how we 'digest' temporality will determine our attitude toward knowledge. William James expressed a profound understanding of the nature of modern knowledge when he wrote that: 'The most significant characteristic of modern civilization is the sacrifice of the future for the present, and all the power of science has been prostituted for this purpose.'³ In this passage James links the concepts of knowledge and that of historical creativity and suggests that, in the Modern Age, there is an abundance of the former and deficit of the latter. We will return to this point in a few moments.

For now let us observe that when Jesus speaks of hunger, he speaks not only of the most obvious constraints to our physical life, but also to the 'hunger' to which words themselves point. If words address the hunger in man, when they express a limit which opens to the infinite, they can almost always meet with receptivity *on some level.* Where there is no hunger there can be no receptivity. 'Cast not your pearls before swine, lest they turn and rend you.' (Matt.7:6) Incommunicability is repletion. The 'pearls' we form in our temporal existence are predicated in some way upon the fact that we have hunger, that we are not replete, that our knowledge is partial.

Jesus's renunciation and practical kenosis assist in bringing man into a communicable condition. Thinking has little actually to do with the intellect. Thinking is hunger for communication.

The Master in the Open Air

In all the millions of words that have been written about Jesus, it must seem daring to add any more and to think that anything new can be said. But perhaps in some of the things that have already been said, we can come up with a slightly different emphasis.

Jesus is someone who appears to spend a lot of time outdoors. He is a master in the open air, walking up and down hills, going out on the water, returning to land, going towards and away from villages and towns, and usually in conversation with others. The conversations of Jesus deal with mountains, clouds, wells, trees, pigs, sheep, lilies, sparrows, seeds, grass. Jesus and the earth appear to speak the same language. Of course, he goes into buildings, temples, and houses, but on the whole as a philosopher, he is a remarkable outdoorsman.

Luke says that he was born in a stable — a place exposed to the elements. He was baptized in a gorge; he was tempted in a desert; his dying occurred on a hill near Jerusalem. Not even death, the ultimate 'being insideness,' could confine him. He returns 'in the clouds' to a humanity confined within four walls.

This pastoral Jesus, this Jesus as the Good Shepherd, has been a theme of innumerable discourses and religious meditations. The events of his life almost have the character of natural phenomena — tornado? earthquake? — except that they are willed, lived, anticipated, expected, consented. Yet they are not 'natural' but 'historical' phenomena. With the genealogical covenant at his back, the open air around him, and his future as history, Jesus goes striding along the landscape, which, in some equally unfathomable way, has been gathered up with him into a language of story and meaning.

The Meta-narrative of Ultra-Realism

Realism says that the things in the world, the data of experience, are 'really there.' 'The terms of [our] understanding are dictated by the way things are.'[4] Polkinghorne defends this realism in science, in particular over against the principle of idealism in modern philosophy, which attributed from the beginning 'a superiority ... to inner experience, by virtue of which knowledge in the outer world becomes problematic.'[5] Elsewhere Polkinghorne comments that '... all forms of realism are divinely underwritten, for God will not mislead us, either in his revelation of himself or in the works of his creation.'[6]

Just how is this divine underwriting accomplished in Christian theology? What is the ultra-realism of the Jesus narrative?

A curious comment by Ludwig Wittgenstein (1889–1951) opens a window into the theology of ultra-realism. When modern philosophy, with its attribution of superiority to inner experience, had become entrenched, language became an important philosophical concern. How do we express our relation to the world? Is language reliable? Without relation, without shared or constant meaning, we should all become solipsists. Solipsism — *solus ipsus,* 'self alone' — says that 'I alone' is real. It is a kind of last-ditch idealism, a withdrawal into the fortress of the self and snapping shut of every bridge, gate, and portcullis. It would not seem to be a very fruitful position to take, rather an indication that all adventure has been exhausted in the struggle to maintain a mere self-defence.

Nevertheless, Wittgenstein saw the possibility for a kind of ultimate solipsism which would be the equivalent of pure realism when (as recorded in A.J. Ayer's *Wittgenstein,* a philosophical biography) he remarked that, '... solipsism, when its implications are followed out strictly, coincides with pure realism. The self of solipsism shrinks to a point without extension and there remains the reality co-ordinated with it.'

This guarantee of ultra-realism became the philosophical nugget of Christian theology, expressed in the high plenitudes of the opening lines of St John's Gospel. The 'I' of Christ is the ground of the world, and humankind's guarantee against all solipsism is in its universal participation in this 'I.' From the One, from the *solus,* it is possible to get to the many by simple addition. The decision to be added to the Story by means of participation rests with each individual — a 'free choice' by definition.

Jesus's repudiation of Satan at the Temptation — 'Get thee behind me, Satan!' — has been turned into a theology of choice: 'Choose Jesus!' By choosing Jesus, the idea was that people would be able to resist the temptation of complete knowledge, that they would 'save' *in* themselves and *for* themselves a kind of hunger that leads to historical creativity. This knowledge which is so tempting, which is so alluring, brings everything to know, everything to choose from, it sprouts into a wonder of possibilities.[7] But: *how to realize? how to bring into fruition?* These are the all-important questions. Jesus's reply to the Tempter, 'Man does not live by bread alone,' abuts the limited to the infinite to make possible the historical.

The Christological idea, Jesus as world-ransom, is an epistemological communion for the adventure which is history.

Epilogue

The Problem of Knowledge

We have come a long way from Moses and the Serpent. Our journey through history and the Bible returns us to this image, which so dramatically portrays the situation of modern man with respect to knowledge.

In reviewing the way we have come, let us return briefly to those 'Appearances' mentioned in Chapter One — those 'Appearances' first of the regularities of the heavens, but then later generally of 'the way things are,' which spoke of a universe seemingly indifferent to human concern and participation. An important moment in this notion of an indifferent universe was reached in the eighteenth century, when the repercussions of the mechanical view of nature reached the borderlands of ethics and philosophy. If the Appearances — the way things are — are indifferent to human life, then it is not possible to deduce any moral guidance whatsoever from them. This philosophical position — called 'No ought from is' — was stated by Hume and resisted by Kant, who went on to make an argument for morality based upon reason. According to Alastair MacIntyre, the dilemma posed by 'No ought from is' formed the essence of the attempt, by eighteenth century philosophers, to rescue morality.[1] In their own way, they were trying to 'save the appearances,' but philosophy no longer possessed a concept of Nature or of Human Nature which would favour such a rescue mission.

Let us continue with our review — our backward scroll through this book. In Chapters Two through Five, I attempted to sketch what I believe Genesis has to tell about Nature and Human Nature. In the 'two-leg theory of human cognition' — the genealogical and the metaphysical — the attempt was made to point out

that *what* thinkers say about man and *when* and *how* they frame
their theories about man are complementary questions. The
'what' is the science and the 'when' and the 'how' are the history,
and no longer, it seems, are we permitted the indulgence of emphasizing the former and neglecting the latter.

The discussion about Jesus converged on the issue of history
and historical consciousness. With Jesus we come to what appears to be a sharp break in the narrative concerning the Covenant
of Abraham and the Law of Moses. With Jesus, this Covenant is
apocalyptically opened up for all believers; and as for the Law, almost all Christians have believed that 'Moses rescued the people
by lifting up a serpent; God does the same through Jesus by lifting him up on the cross.'[2]

It has not been my purpose in this book to discuss the dissimilarities that exist between the Mosaic Law and the Christian
Gospel. These dissimilarities (as well as similarities) exist. My
aim has been directed at the problem of knowledge rather than
that of Law and Gospel. On the problem of knowledge I think that
Jews and Christians would find profound kinship.

For today, we are a long way from the eighteenth century confidence in 'the way things are.' Our *is* — the historical reality in
which we are immersed — has been shaken by the pace and acceleration of knowledge. In our information-based society,
knowledge has become not only a commodity. It is a marker of
wealth and poverty, health and sickness, life and death. The question of 'ought' has come to the forefront. No longer can we blind
ourselves to the ethical consequences of our knowledge.

Thus we are living through a strange reversal of the dictum,
'No ought from is.' Indeed it is impossible to consider the problem of knowledge in the late twentieth century without being confronted with ethics. Should human life be extended? Should the
Human Genome Project go forward without restraint? Should
women advertise their eggs over the Internet? Does the sheer
flood-tide of information and alternatives available to us over-
whelm the faculty of reflective thought, or cripple the moral
sense? How does all of this intellectually-derived abundance
affect our ability to act — an ability which often depends on more
limited, even stubborn, convictions?

Thus it is not only legitimate to ask if there are things *we ought not to know*.[3] Certainly 'oughtness' — matters of right and wrong — touches upon our knowledge in this direct way. But in the larger sense, the problem of knowledge and the problem of history (to put it in those broad terms) begin to seem inextricably connected. Given in the realm of the 'ought' (ethical questions) which we confront in almost any venture of modern knowledge, there is an *is:* which is our existence as historical beings, our historical condition.

The picture of Moses with the Serpent goes to the heart of modernity's new encounter with the ought/is dilemma. Moses grasps the symbol of the Tempter in this form, the Tempter whose Greek name is *diaballein*. And just as the lifting up of the Serpent leads through historical development to the lifting up of Jesus on the Cross, there is an historical development to be seen in the treatment of the problem of knowledge which leads from Moses through Christ to the present day. But it has not yet been resolved in the sense that the Cross resolved certain problems of the Law and the Covenant.

Our unresolved problem is that knowledge and *diaballein* accompany us through life. Both as seekers of knowledge and as participants in historical existence, we experience the sting of the serpent's venom. We could no more dispense with knowledge than we could with history. Our inescapable task is learning how to *consecrate* the venom.

For if it is true that Knowledge and the Serpent's Venom accompany us through history, in gaining knowledge we need to learn how to handle the temptations. For this, biblical epistemology, with its complex view of human origins, its uncompromising intellectual honesty, and its teachings of patience, fruitfulness, and limits, is indispensable.

For it may be, on some mythical Last Day, that we will come to some final Judgment. By then, let us hope, we will have learned the secrets of the *consecration of the venom* — recapitulating the steps, through history, to the Tree of Life. For *that* fruit was always permitted.

Endnotes

Introduction

1. 'And when Abram was ninety years old and nine, the Lord appeared to Abram and said unto him, *I am* the Almighty God, walk before me and be thou perfect. And I will make my covenant between me and thee, and will multiply thee exceedingly ...' Gen.17:1,2
2. Some examples: 'And he spoke many things unto them in parables ...' Matt.13:3
   'And all these things spake Jesus unto the multitude in parables; and without a parable spake he not unto them ...' Matt.13:34
   'And he said unto them, Know ye not this parable? and how then will ye know all parables?' Mark 4:13
   'And he said, Unto you it is given to know the mysteries of God: but to others in parables; that seeing they might not see, and hearing they might not understand.' Luke 8:10.
3. And that of Thomas Aquinas. 'In the work of Thomas Aquinas, in particular, the word *participate* or *participation* occurs on almost every page, and a whole book could be written — indeed one has been written — on the uses he makes of it. It is not a technical term of philosophy and he is no more concerned to define it than a modern philosopher would be, to define some such common tool of his thought as, say, the word compare.' Owen Barfield, *Saving the Appearances: A Study in Idolatry,* New York 1965, p.89.
4. Russell Kirk, *op. cit.,* 1995, p.166.
5. John Lukacs, *Historical Consciousness,* New York 1968, p.40.
6. Sheldon Hackney, 'Higher Education as a Medium for Culture,' *American Behavioral Scientist,* vol.42, no.6, March 1999.
7. From a note in the Scofield Reference Bible: 'The serpent, in his Edenic form, is not to be thought of as a writhing reptile. That is the effect of the curse (Gen.3:14) The creature which lent itself to Satan may well have been the most beautiful as it was the most "subtle" of creatures less than man ... In the serpent, Satan first appeared as "an angel of light".'(2 Cor.11:1)

Chapter One

1. Dietrich Bonhoeffer, *Creation and Fall; Temptation: Two Biblical Studies,* New York 1959, p.52.
2. Leo Strauss, 'On the Interpretation of Genesis,' *L'Homme,* janv–mars, 1981, XXI(1), p.5.
3. Bonhoeffer, *op. cit.,* p.65f.
4. Hermann Poppelbaum, *A New Zoology,* Philosophic-Anthroposophic Press, Dornach 1961, p.93.
5. Poppelbaum, *op. cit.,* pp.93–95.
6. Owen Barfield, *Saving the Appearances,* 1965, p.161.
7. There seems to be a sort of 'double movement' involved with imagination, a kind of 'as-if' experience. Those who wish to pursue it may find Barfield's characterization of the double-step relevant: 'To be *able* to experience the representations as idols, and then to be able to perform the act of figuration consciously, so as to be able to experience them as participated: that is imagination.' *Saving the Appearances,* p. 147. To explain what Barfield means by 'act of figuration' would take us too far afield, but the sense of a 'double movement' is very evident in this passage.
8. 'The middle voice of the Greek verb suggests neither wholly "what is perceived, from within themselves, by men," nor wholly "what, from without, forces itself on man's senses," but something between the two. This is also fairly suggested by the English word "appearances," which is generally used in translating the once hard-worked phrase *sozein ta phainomena* — "to save the appearances." This phrase, used by Simplicius in his sixth century *Commentary* on Aristotle's *De Caelo,* continued to dominate astronomy down to the time of Copernicus.' Barfield, p.48
9. Barfield, *op. cit.,* p.161.
10. John Lukacs, *Historical Consciousness,* New York 1968, p.5.
11. Lukacs, *op. cit.,* p.5.

Chapter Two

1. Stanley L. Jaki, *Genesis I Through the Ages,* Thomas More Press, 1992, p.299.
2. Jaki, *op.cit.,* p.89.
3. Jaki, *op. cit.,* p.52.
4. Jaki, *op. cit.,* p.22.
5. Jaki has an interesting discussion on the Hebrew word *bara,* translated 'created.' He says the Hebrew word 'means basically "to split" and "to slash" or an action which conveys that something is divided

and that the action is done swiftly ... In the overwhelming number of its Old Testament uses *bara* conveys the notion that God did something with marvellous ease and speed.' *op.cit.,* p.5.
6. Walker Percy, 'The Mystery of Language,' in *The Message in the Bottle,* New York 1975, p.155.

Chapter Three

1. The Hebrew word for 'image,' as in the 'Image of God' (in which man was created: Gen.1:26) is *tselem,* meaning 'shade' or 'shadow.' (From Leon Kass)
2. 'For He had now only one name — I AM — and that was participated by every being who had eyes that saw and ears that heard and who spoke through his throat. But it was incommunicable, because its participation by the particular self which is at this moment uttering it was an inseparable part of its meaning. Everyone can call his idol "God," and many do; but no being who speaks through his throat can call a wholly other and outer Being "I".' Owen Barfield, *Saving the Appearances,* p.114.
3. Emil Bock, *Moses,* Edinburgh 1986, p.82.
4. *The Oxford Companion to the Mind,* Richard L. Gregory, ed., Oxford 1987, p.800.
5. From Søren Kierkegaard's *The Concept of Irony,* quoted by A. Delbanco in *The Death of Satan,* New York 1995, p.202.
6. Compare 'The concept of meaning is every bit as problematic as the concept of mind, and for related reasons. For it seems to be the case that *only for a mind* that some things (gestures, sounds, marks, or natural phenomena) can *mean* other things ... Anyone who conceives of science as objective, and of objectivity as requiring the study of phenomena (objects and the relations between objects) which exist, and have their character independently of human thought, will face a problem with the scientific study of meaning.' *Oxford Companion to the Mind,* p.450f.
7. From *The Philosophical Works of Descartes,* Vol.1, Cambridge University Press, 1911, p.101.

Chapter Four

1. Ortega y Gasset, *Man and Crisis,* Norton, 1958, p.216.
2. Of course there has been a tremendous historical development in rational thought. Thinkers have built on each other's work over time. But only rarely has history itself been an element of the

thought itself, an epistemological reality, an epistemological condition itself.

3. More recently Michel Foucault, in his essay "What is an author?"
abolished the concept of original authorship, replacing it with 'function of discourse.' He wrote: 'How, under what conditions, and in
what forms, can something like a subject appear in the order of discourse? What place can it occupy in each type of discourse, what
functions can it assume, and by obeying what rules? In short, *it is a
matter of depriving the subject (or its substitute) of its role as originator, and of analysing the subject as a variable and complex function of discourse.*' (Italics mine.) Quoted in R.V. Young's 'New
Historicism: Literature and the Will to Power,' *The Intercollegiate
Review,* Vol.31, No.1, Fall, 1995.

4. An example of the increasing politicization of society. What might
once have been occasion for a lesson in good manners has become an
issue of political ideology.

5. Ortega y Gasset, *The Revolt of the Masses,* New York 1932, p.72.

6. Compare John Lukacs: 'Our purposes are more important than our
motives.' And: 'Anticipation leaps across past and present. And thus
"the pull of the future" may function as a "cause," a component of
events. That which will be is to some extent the cause of that which
is ... We are not merely the products of the past; we are also creators
of the future ... Hence the inadequacy of the still prevalent concept of
mechanical causality as it depends on the absolutely irreversible
sequence of time ...' From his discussion 'Thinking about Causes,' in
Historical Consciousness, 1968, p.158f.

Chapter Five

1. Compare Alastair MacIntyre: 'Our biological nature certainly places
constraints on all cultural possibility; but man who has nothing but a
biological nature is a creature of whom we know nothing.' *After
Virtue,* 1984, p.161.

2. Susanne K. Langer, *Philosophy in a New Key,* Harvard 1979, p.108f.

3. Compare Walter Lippmann: 'The disesteem into which moralists
have fallen is due at bottom to their failure to see that in an age like
this one the function of the moralist is not to exhort men to be good
but to elucidate what the good is.' *A Preface to Morals,* 1929, p.318.

4. Roger Lewin, *Bones of Contention,* New York 1987, p.319.

5. I personally think that it must have been a breakthrough discovery in
human evolution when man discovered that he could *walk and think
at the same time.* This seems so obvious for us, yet what we take for
granted may represent an enormous step (literally) forward. Look to

the religious traditions for evidence. Deep meditation is facilitated by the sitting posture. A faint echo of *walking and thinking together* survives in the philosophical tradition. From Aristotle to Kant, philosophers have sometimes been known as steady walkers. I offer this idea half-seriously — but in the spirit of trying to provoke thought concerning simple, common occurrences.

6. 'I believe that human beings are "essentially" neotenous, not because I can enumerate a list of important paedomorphic features, but because *a general, temporal redardation of development has clearly characterized human evolution.This redardation established a matrix within which all trends in the evolution of human morphology must be assessed.*' (Italics his.) Stephen Jay Gould, *Ontogeny and Phylogeny*, Harvard 1977, p.365.

7. Gould, *op. cit.*, above, p.402.

8. A relevant saying from the gnostic Christians: 'The Ancient of Eternity is ever a child,' also expresses the neotenous idea.

9. Himmelfarb, *op. cit.*, p.167.

10. 'Any analysis of the *Origin*, like the history of its background, is plagued by the confusion between the theory of evolution (what Darwin called the "theory of descent") and the theory of natural selection (p.312) ... Not only the concept of the survival of the fittest but even that of the struggle for existence has been found to be less obvious and more dubious than might seem to be the case at first sight (p.316) ... The undisciplined nature of Darwin's concept of adaptation (p.318) ... There would be no objections to such hypothetical reasons, if they merely served to establish the consistency of the hypothesis. But what they establish is less its consistency than its plasticity, the ease with which it can be bent into any desired shape (p.319) ... If in one respect natural selection may be criticized for trying to explain too much; in another, it may be thought to explain too little (p.321) ...' and so on. These are samples of some of Himmelfarb's critiques of Darwin. From her *Darwin and the Darwinian Revolution*, Chicago 1962.

Chapter Six

1. Compare Susan Haack, in her *Evidence and Inquiry: Towards Reconstruction in Epistemology*, Blackwell Publishers, 1993, 1995: 'There is no reason to deny that there are important cognitive capacities which are pre-propositional, in the sense both that they are necessary conditions of a creature's having propositional knowledge, and that they may be shared by adult humans and human infants ... Nor is there any reason to deny that there are many things people can

do which they cannot articulate how to do — ride a bicycle or recognize a face, for instance.' (p.169)

2. Rudolf Steiner, *The Philosophy of Freedom*, 1964, p.41.

3. Emil Bock, *Genesis*, Edinburgh 1983, p.49.

4. The relation of 'participatory cognition' to conception is far from understood today. In a recent television documentary on human infertility, it was said that 1.2 million Americans seek medical assistance for problems relating to reproduction. This is a vast number of people. Infertility has always existed. But is a sharp increase in it characteristic of modernity?

5. Emil Bock, *Genesis: Creation and the Patriarchs*, Edinburgh 1983, p.51.

6. See Introduction and Chapter One.

7. *Oxford Companion to the Mind*, ed. Richard Gregory, Oxford 1987, p.601.

8. 'Percept' is usefully defined by Rudolf Steiner: 'It is, then, not the *process* of observation but the *object* of observation which I call the "percept".' Steiner, *op. cit.*, p.44.

9. Oliver Sacks, *The Man Who Mistook His Wife for a Hat*, New York 1987, p.12.

10. Dr P. was only able to make the connection when he *smelled* the rose. This fact, too, carries with it much revelatory richness. Remember, God breathed into man the breath of life through his *nostrils*. In some Jewish legends, it is said that it is through smell that man knows the difference between right and wrong, good and evil — that smelling is the one sense-capacity that does not deceive us.

11. Emil Bock, *op. cit.*, p.50.

Chapter Seven

1. Alvin Plantinga, 'The Free Will Defence,' in *Philosophy of Religion*, Oxford University Press, 1996, p.270.

2. Compare Lev Shestov: '... it was precisely the fruits of the tree of knowledge which lulled the human mind to sleep.' And: [the biblical story of the tree of knowledge] is 'the only true critique of pure reason that has ever been formulated on this earth.' *Athens and Jerusalem*, trans. Bernard Martin, Ohio University Press, 1966, p.255.

3. Lev Shestov, *op. cit.*, p.307.

4. Eugene Rosenstock-Huessy, *Judaism Despite Christianity*, University of Alabama, 1969, p.81.

5. A concept which it would be useful to examine — 'if we have the time!' I believe that for the ancient Hebrews, 'waste of time' was

something akin to a horror, something idolatrous, unclean.
6. Science still does not know all the causes for infertility. Jill Smolowe, a journalist who struggled for years to conceive, remarked in her book, *The Empty Lap,* that: 'even with everything in working order, the odds of a woman conceiving in any given month are just one in four. Factor in any of the ugly-sounding problems that can arise ... and it begins to seem that the *real* freaks are the women who manage to get pregnant without benefit of needles, vials, or petri dishes.'
7. Commenting on these two lines in Genesis, Vladimir Solovyev wrote: 'The individual mind is here not merely the organ of personal existence, but likewise the organ of remembrance and divination for the whole of humanity, and even for the whole of Nature. The Hebrew who wrote: *This is the book of the generation of the heavens and the earth,* and farther: *This is the book of the generations of man,* was expressing not only his personal and national consciousness. Through him first shone forth in the world the truth of the unity of the whole universe and of all mankind. And all further advances in knowledge consist solely in the development and embodiment of this truth, for the reason that it is impossible for consciousness to go beyond this universal form.' *The Meaning of Love,* London 1945, p.19.
8. Compare: The pitiable case of child beauty star Jon Benét Ramsey: 'Imposed upon her childish innocence like a lurid mask is a look of sexual precocity.' See 'Who Killed Jon Benét Ramsey?' by Joyce Carol Oates, in *The New York Review of Books,* June 24, 1999.
9. Silvano Arieti, *Abraham and the Contemporary Mind,* New York 1981, p.129, 130.
10. Kierkegaard contrasts the Knight of Faith with the tragic hero: 'The tragic hero relinquishes himself in order to express the universal; the knight of faith relinquishes the universal in order to become the single individual.' *Fear and Trembling,* Princeton 1983, p.75.
11. Shestov, *op. cit.,* p.244.
12. Arieti, *op. cit.,* p.139.
13. Compare John Lukacs: '... the past, too, is something that cannot be stowed away into a simple, definite, closed category ... Death and the past are not the same. Death is irrevocable; the past is not. And, if death and the past are not the same, life and the present are not the same either. The present is an abstract illusion, the elusive and slightly sickening sensation of past and future meeting in our minds; but life, unlike the present, is not an illusion at all ... Thus, in a sense, it is life and the past that belong together; and, in another sense, it is death and the present: for death is not the freezing of the past, it is the freezing of the present.' *Historical Consciousness,* 1968 ed., p.35.

14. Louis Sass, 'Surface and Depth: Wittgenstein's Reflections on Psychoanalysis,' *Partisan Review* #4, 1998.
15. Susanne K. Langer, *Philosophy in a New Key,* Harvard 1984, p.41.
16. From the Latin *secare,* 'to cut.'
17. '... [Kant] was shaken from his "dogmatic slumber" by Hume, who demonstrated that precisely the constitutive Forms of the conceptional knowledge of reality, especially the Form of causality, are not given in perception, but are products of the mechanism of association without any demonstrable relation to the real.' And in a note: 'The dogmatism from which, therefore, Kant declared that he had been freed through Hume *was that of empiricism.*' Wilhelm Windelband, *A History of Philosophy,* Vol.II, New York 1958, p.537.
18. Windelband: '*A priori* is, with Kant ... means not a chronological priority to experience, but *a universality and necessity of validity in principles of reason which really transcends all experience ...*' (Italics his). *op. cit.,* p.534.
19. Walker Percy commenting on Ernst Cassirer, in his 'Semiotic and a Theory of Knowledge,' in *The Message in the Bottle,* New York 1975, p.262.
20. Walker Percy, 'Symbol as Hermeneutic in Existentialism,' *op. cit.,* p.283.

Chapter Eight

1. See George Adam Smith, *The Historical Geography of the Holy Land,* London 1897, p.47. And p.103: 'By numerous little tokens, we feel that this is a scenery described by ... men who ... looked down upon their prospects and painted their scenes from above. Their usual word for valley is *depth* — something below them; for terror and destruction some of their commonest names mean originally *abyss.*'
2. Paul de Man, *Allegories of Reading,* Yale 1979, p.111.
3. Quoted by Eugene Rosenstock-Huessy, *The Christian Future,* 1946, following p.57.
4. John Polkinghorne, *One World,* Princeton 1986, p.22.
5. Wilhelm Windelband, *A History of Philosophy,* Vol.II, New York 1958, p.466. (Original italicized.)
6. Polkinghorne, *The Faith of a Physicist,* Princeton 1994, p.156.
7. Every historical age specializes, and every period gains its distinction at the price of something else. A period of metaphysical philosophy will probably not be a period of scientific innovation and technological change. Nevertheless the peculiar character of the modern situation in history is expressed in the New Testament temptation story. This is more than the normal see-saw of talents and inclinations lead-

ing to specialization in certain areas and crudeness or poverty in others. In its ambition for complete knowledge, modernity may represent a particular form of temptation, and one that puts strain on the process of history itself.

Epilogue

1. See his *After Virtue,* Notre Dame 1984, pp.55–59.
2. Frank Thielman, *The Law and the New Testament: The Question of Continuity,* Crossroad Publishing, New York 1998, p.179. The reference is to John 3:14–15.
3. See Roger Shattuck, *Forbidden Knowledge: From Prometheus to Pornography,* (New York 1996) which is an extended treatment of this theme. He quotes a scientist, Nicholas Rescher: 'There are various things we simply ought not to know. If we did not have to live our lives amidst a fog of uncertainty about a whole range of matters that are actually of fundamental interest and importance to us, it would no longer be a human mode of existence that we would live. Instead we would become a being of another sort, perhaps angelic, perhaps machine-like, but certainly not human.' (p.43)

Further Reading

Arieti, Silvano, *Abraham and the Contemporary Mind,* Basic Books, New York 1981.

Armstrong, Karen, *In the Beginning,* A. Knopf, New York 1996.

Barfield, Owen, *Saving the Appearances: A Study in Idolatry,* New York 1965.

—, *History, Guilt, and Habit,* Wesleyan University Press 1979.

—, *Romanticism Comes of Age,* Wesleyan University Press 1986.

Bock, Emil, *Moses,* Floris Books, Edinburgh 1986.

—, *Genesis:: Creation and the Patriarchs,* Floris Books, Edinburgh 1983.

—, *The Three Years,* Christian Community Press 1959; rep. Floris Books, Edinburgh 1994.

Bonhoeffer, Dietrich, *Creation and Fall; Temptation: Two Biblical Studies,* New York 1959.

Delbanco, Andrew, The Death of Satan, Farrar, Straus & Giroux, New York 1995.

de Man, Paul, *Allegories of Reading,* Yale 1979.

Descartes, René, *The Philosophical Works of Descartes,* Vol.1, Cambridge University Press 1911.

Eldredge, Niles and Ian Tattersall, *The Myths of Human Evolution,* Columbia University Press, 1982.

Eliot, T.S. *Christianity and Culture,* Harcourt-Brace, New York 1977.

Gould, Stephen Jay, *Ontogeny and Phylogeny,* Harvard 1977.

Gregory, Richard L. Ed., *The Oxford Companion to the Mind,* Oxford 1987.

Haack, Susan, *Evidence and Inquiry: Towards Reconstruction in Epistemology,* Blackwell Publishers 1995.

Hackney, Sheldon, 'Higher Education as a Medium for Culture,' *American Behavioral Scientist,* Vol.42, no.6, March 1999.

Heisenberg, Werner, *Philosophical Problems of Quantum Physics,* Woodbridge, Connecticut 1979.

Himmelfarb, Gertrude, *Darwin and the Darwinian Revolution,* Chicago 1962.

Jaki, Stanley L. *Genesis 1 Through the Ages,* Thomas More Press 1992.

Kierkegaard, Søren, *Fear and Trembling,* Princeton 1983.

Kirk, Russell, *The Sword of Imagination,* Eerdman's Publishers, Grand Rapids, Mich. 1995.

Langer, Susanne K. *Philosophy in a New Key,* Harvard 1979.

Lewin, Roger, *Bones of Contention,* New York 1987.

Lieberman, Philip, *The Biology and Evolution of Language,* Harvard 1984.

Lippmann, Walter, *A Preface to Morals,* Macmillan, New York 1929.

Lukacs, John, *Historical Consciousness,* Harper & Row, New York 1968; 1985.

—, *Confessions of an Original Sinner,* Ticknor & Fields, New York 1990.

—, *The End of the Twentieth Century and the End of the Modern Age,* Ticknor & Fields, New York 1993.

MacIntyre, Alastair, *After Virtue,* Notre Dame 1984.

Man, Paul de, *Allegories of Reading,* Yale 1979.

Mead, G.R.S. *Fragments of a Faith Forgotten,* University Books, New Hyde Park, New York 1960.

Needleman, Jacob, *Lost Christianity,* Dorset 1990.

Ortega y Gasset, José, *Man and Crisis,* Norton, New York 1958.

—, *The Revolt of the Masses,* New York 1932.

—, *What Is Philosophy?* New York 1960.

—, *Man and People,* New York 1957.

—, *History as a System,* New York 1961.

—, *Some Lessons in Metaphysics,* New York 1970.

Percy, Walker, 'The Mystery of Language,' in *The Message in the Bottle,* New York 1975.

Plantinga, Alvin, 'The Free Will Defence,' in *Philosophy of Religion,* Oxford University Press 1996.

Polkinghorne, John, *The Faith of a Physicist,* Princeton 1994.

—, *One World,* Princeton 1986.

Poppelbaum, Hermann, *A New Zoology,* Philosophic–Anthroposophic Press, Dornach 1961.

Rosenstock-Huessy, Eugene, *Judaism Despite Christianity,* University of Alabama, Tuscaloosa, Alabama 1969.

—, *The Christian Future,* New York 1946.

Sacks, Oliver, *The Man Who Mistook His Wife for a Hat,* New York 1987.

Shestov, Lev, *Athens and Jerusalem,* trans. Bernard Martin, Ohio University Press 1966.

Solovyev, Vladimir, *The Meaning of Love,* London 1945.

—, *A Short Narrative of the Anti-Christ,* St George Publications.

Smith, George Adam, *The Historical Geography of the Holy Land,* London 1897.

Steiner, George, *No Passion Spent,* New Haven 1996.

Steiner, Rudolf, *The Philosophy of Freedom,* London 1964.

—, *The Secrets of the Biblical Story of Creation,* Health Research Reprint 1971.

—, *The Influences of Lucifer and Ahriman: Man's Responsibility for the Earth,* Steiner Book Centre, Vancouver, Canada 1984.

—, *The Gospel of St. John,* Anthroposophic Press 1962.

Strauss, Leo, 'On the Interpretation of Genesis,' *L'Homme,* janv–mars 1981, XXI(1).

Thielman, Frank, *The Law and the New Testament: The Question of Continuity,* Crossroad Publishing, New York 1998.

Tinder, Glenn, *The Political Meaning of Christianity,* Harper San Francisco, 1989.

Walsh, William, *The Use of Imagination,* Barnes & Noble, New York 1959.

Weaver, Richard M. *Ideas Have Consequences,* Chicago University Press 1948.

Windelband, Wilhelm, *A History of Philosophy,* Vol.II, New York 1958.

Manuscript collection

Papers of John Lukens. Birmingham Public Library Archives, Birmingham, Alabama.

Index